AI: GAME ON

HOW TO DECIDE WHO OR WHAT DECIDES

Leveraging the predictive power of
artificial intelligence for your organisation

Tim Trumper

Visit the AI: Game On website for live links and updates
http://aigameon.com

Published in 2024 by Hardie Grant Books an imprint of Hardie Grant Publishing

Hardie Grant Books (Melbourne)
Ground Floor, Building 1, 658 Church Street
Richmond VIC 3121, Australia

www.hardiegrant.com.au

Hardie Grant acknowledges the Traditional Owners of the Country on which we work, the Wurundjeri People of the Kulin Nation and the Gadigal People of the Eora Nation, and recognises their continuing connection to the land, waters and culture. We pay our respects to their Elders past and present.

A catalogue record of this book is available from the National Library of Australia.
AI: Game On

ISBN 9781761450839

FSC
www.fsc.org
MIX
Paper from responsible sources
FSC® C009448

Publication commissioned by Courtney Nicholls
Publication managed by Hannah Louey
Cover and internal design by Cupcake Design Studio
Typeset by Michelle Pirovich
Printed in Australia by Ellikon Fine Printers

To Elizabeth, Syd and Anna.

Thank you for:

The wonders we have seen.

The people we are fortunate to know.

The adventures that await.

ABOUT TIM TRUMPER

Tim is Chairman of the NRMA, an advisor to and a founding shareholder in Quantium, which provides data and analytics to some of the world's leading brands, and he also holds interests in several private high-growth innovative companies, including andi search.

His career has spanned diverse categories including artificial intelligence and machine learning, big data, digital transformation, mobility and transport, financial services and media.

He is an authority on the utilisation of data to drive innovation and corporate strategy. His core interest relates to how business leaders facilitate successful AI and machine-learning business transformation to drive innovation, for corporate strategy and for the service of customers and the community.

Tim is an experienced chair, non-executive director, former CEO, and advisor to high-performance global and Australian companies.

He holds an MBA from UNE and in 2018 completed Harvard's Making Corporate Boards More Effective Governance Program, and is a graduate of AICD.

CONTENTS

PREFACE

A wise man said to me a long time ago, there is never a good time to build a house, have a child, start a business, or write a book. The book is last on this list for me, and it's been a long time coming. Thank you, Jaqui Lane and Michael Parker, for helping me through it all.

My journey into data started a long time ago when I was fortunate to meet amazing pioneers of the internet Louis Rossetto and Jane Metcalfe, the pair who in 1993 co-founded *Wired* magazine in their San Francisco offices. It set me up for a long journey in the world of data and analytics and how it can be used to understand and predict intention and attention, the two new asset classes of our time. Rossetto and Metcalfe talked about what they saw coming at the near dawn of the World Wide Web. Australia at that time had a few hundred email users, and a handful of real working websites that were not just green screen text.

Think about what has changed in those three decades. Pretty much everything has changed.

Louis pointed to a copy of the San Francisco Yellow Pages and said, 'This is worthless.' At the time Yellow Pages was a massive industry. He went on to say, 'If you can work out who will need medical help or buy a new car this weekend in San Francisco it is close to priceless. What we are building here is a way to know everything.' He was talking about a prediction machine, and it blew my mind. Louis saw the need for search, before AltaVista, Yahoo, Google, Andi and others. It was an amazing prediction.

Then in 1997 the head of Microsoft strategy in Seattle said to me, 'Everybody knows that the guy with the best data on their customers' needs will win,' as he explained how in the dial-up world they were trying to understand hundreds of millions of customers' interactions with Word. In 1997 this was a mind-blowing initiative.

I spent many years looking for what would come out of this line of thinking about large-scale data sets.

I worked in the media for many years, using what data we had to best inform strategy. It was low-grade data from surveys and focus groups. We did our best with it. When the internet really fired up it was a game changer.

Then in 2009 I met Adam Driussi, co-founder and now CEO of Quantium. I was helping an insurance company at that time and Adam made a pitch to the board. Adam has a very sharp mind and combines this with a passion for helping companies find real scaled insights and increasingly apply AI-enabled actions to their data.

Having seen hundreds of pitches to companies, I was taken with what Adam put forward. What he showed was powerful. By using de-identified credit card data it enabled the understanding of real customer behaviours of the insurance company customers; not surveyed, and not a small sample, it was scaled and the behaviours were real.

What was most interesting was how you could use this data to work out why customers defected. Was it price, service, poor claims, or something else? The nuances in the real use of data were ground-breaking. The client company bought the offering and it helped transform it at that time.

I found it so interesting I followed up with Adam and after a few conversations I joined Quantium as a shareholder and advisor. Quantium has grown from those days, when there were about 14 people, to become a global business with over 1,200 staff today. This journey with Quantium has allowed me to work with very smart people and to learn a great deal about the frontiers of data use, analytics and AI deployment. As you read this book it will become clear that much of my perspective is informed by my relationship with Quantium and no doubt osmosis has been hard at work over many years. Being in the practice of analytics and knowing the governance concerns of boards is not a common combination, so I do hope this perspective is helpful for the reader.

The first prompt for writing this book was from a CEO client of mine, who said, 'You've had a front-row seat at the forefront of data use, AI enablement and data ethics for over three decades – why not tell us some of what you have learnt?'

Next, the chair of one of Australia's top 20 companies said to me, 'Tim, you have a unique vantage point, as you are a data practitioner, and also a chair of a very large corporation. You can see a board's perspective on governance, risk and strategy. You can also see the data and use case challenges executives in hundreds of companies all over the world are working on. And you can see their ethical dilemmas. Let others in on what you have learnt.'

The comments above, and many others, stayed with me for years. What has become a blinding flash of the obvious is how the concentration of data use and applications of AI are growing fast, and the advantages of all this analytical firepower have made a few people very wealthy, and left many companies, consumers and social groups behind. The AI data advantages have become concentrated in the hands of a few tech giants at the expense of thousands of companies, and billions of consumers. If I can help change some of this, I should do what I can.

The whole world is increasingly focused on equity, transparency, and a more inclusive orientation. I've written *AI: Game On* to help business leaders who want to thrive in a world that is ever more data-driven and AI-directed. These developments must be properly scrutinised for ethical standards and data use cases.

I have seen many examples of where the data use cases and AI can align to the customer's benefit, and company advantage, while helping society. This should not be a rare event; this should be the way of the future.

Finally, if you've been dismissing AI, applied analytics, machine learning and deep neural networks as not applicable to your business, you'll soon discover your perspective is out of date. And if you've skimmed over these developments as being too hard, you need to know that embracing the world of data and AI is simply not optional. So, for those who harbour doubts, I suggest you suspend your disbelief, and be prepared to accept that what was once science fiction is now fact.

Tim Trumper
January 2024

INTRODUCTION

Data and AI are changing how we think about how we think.

The Turing test (for whether a machine can exhibit intelligent behaviour indistinguishable from that of a human) is redundant now and deemed a low bar in the tech world. We have seen how a particular form of AI using natural language, known as ChatGPT (generative pre-trained transformer), passed the US medical licensing exam, the bar exam, and the Wharton MBA final exam. But bear in mind that it has also prepopulated a lot of false information and is a long way from perfect.

Nonetheless, since its release in late November 2022, ChatGPT reached the 100 million users metric with the fastest adoption rate ever for a new technology platform. It's a sign that the world is at an inflection point – it is AI: Game On.

The advances in AI and generative AI are now so omnipresent that we are surrounded by AI applications that appear to be human and, in many cases, deceive humans.

Up until the early 2020s human beings have been the undisputed best source of knowledge, collectors of data, and the instigators of the most predictive capability in the known universe. From the most basic forms of knowledge, such as where is the next waterhole, and will we have enough food for the winter? Human beings could thrive with only some predictive cognitive ability. It is our superpower that allows us to survive against predators despite their superior physical assets.

Today's highly complex competitive business world boils down to the fact that the more accurately and faster you can predict what is going to happen to your organisation, your customers and your competitors, the more successful your decisions will be today, and that changes your destiny.

Google's CEO called an 'all-hands code red' in December 2022 over the impact of generative AI and the explosion of innovation that is coming via OpenAI's ChatGPT-4 and other AI applications. If Google is worried about what it will do to their business, it may be naive to assume it will not influence every organisation.

We are at the start of a new wave of large innovation that some claim will be the most significant in human history. When platform shifts happen, such as with electricity, cars, television and the internet, the impacts come in waves and the final destination is not clear. We are here now for AI and all leadership teams need to be thinking about what AI: Game On means to them.

Today's world increasingly requires AI literacy, not coding skills. Although coding skills are clearly valuable, leadership teams will need to understand AI's capabilities, risks and the use cases that align with the organisation's purpose and society's expectations. That understanding extends to people's safety, their careers, and equitable aspects of humanity. We are at the time where it is AI: Game On and there is a growing need to navigate the AI systems that are beginning to pervade everyone's lives.

Eric Schmidt, former chair of Alphabet (Google), notes:

> **It's pretty clear to me that there's going to end up being the system that knows everything, and then there's going to be a supervisory system that limits it.**

The founder of a data analytics company in San Francisco said to me, 'There are only four things that you can do with predictive data: find customers, keep customers, understand what they want next from you and optimise your capex towards the future needs of the customer.' All four are mission-critical.

In 2008 Chris Anderson, editor of *Wired*, stated that the 'sheer volume of data would obviate theory and even scientific method.'[1] Many in the business world missed the impact of this thinking and the possibilities he was talking about. Of course, Chris was envisioning a new age of decision-making, one where theory is created and tested, with trillions of variables in seconds – where insights from the market and customers are available at the atomic level for each customer, each action and each non-action. This can lead to the understanding of cause and effect of every input, priced, with likely competitive action mapped and countered in seconds.

In 2023 many more directors, leaders and executives across every part of the economy and society are utilising the power of data in their decision-making, business platforms, research and more. If you're not, you're going to be outpaced or, more plainly, you're toast.

---

1   https://www.wired.com/2008/06/pb-theory/.

We are at the point where a new model of business is evolving. It is one in which the 'data vertebrate' has evolved to dominate the data invertebrate. Capturing signals from the real source of truth, the customer, and having a data spine that helps the organisation to interpret and respond to these signals is what the new predictive organisations are set up to do. Capturing data is one thing; creating an organisation that responds in an ethical way, that aligns with the values of society, is much harder.

This book is not about the tech companies, although there is a lot to be learned by understanding them, and *AI: Game On* will show some of what these companies are doing with AI and data. *AI: Game On* is for you, and how you can use this information for the organisation you are in, or about to join at a board or executive level. As you read about the good, the bad and the ugly experiences that companies are encountering with data and AI, consider whether you and those around you in your company see data and artificial intelligence as material company assets, which will ensure your company is around in the next five to 10 years. Then think about what stage your company (and you) have reached right now in leveraging your data for future growth. Identifying your current position on the data-opportunity continuum is the first step to being in the AI game, the first step towards becoming a predictive company. The benefits of becoming a predictive organisation cannot be overstated.

I have had a front-row seat in seeing how intellectual property and the data infrastructure developed to perpetually understand customers and their behaviours. They are the new crucial company assets, the drivers of enterprise value and opportunity.

Value accrues to those who solve hard problems. Turning your organisation into one that is excellent at harvesting data and using data for the customers' benefit is hard, and it explains, in part, why the value here is currently so concentrated in the tech giants. Research by McKinsey notes that organisations that leverage customer behavioural insights outperform peers by 85% in sales growth and more than 25% in gross margin.[2]

This book is written for those who want to find this new way.

---

2   https://www.mckinsey.com/business-functions/mckinsey-analytics/our-insights/capturing-value-from-your-customer-data.

PART I

THE JOURNEY TO AI: GAME ON

Chapter 1

DATA FLOWS HAVE CHANGED BUSINESS AND THE WORLD

'Everybody knows that the guy with the best data on their customers' needs will win.'[3]

The fabric of the global economy and business has changed in the last three decades. Labour and capital, while still drivers, are now massively augmented with data and IP to create value.

Data, AI and technology are now combining to dramatically outpace labour and capital as the determinates of future economic growth and value. Companies that are enabling the full use of this new combination are out-performing those that have not yet been able to form a cohesive response to AI. Any organisation that is not becoming more data-driven, AI-enabled and customer-centric is borrowing against its future. Google CEO Sundar Pichai describes AI as 'the most profound technology we are working on today' and Microsoft CEO Satya Nadella said, 'I have not seen something like this since I would say 2007–2008 when the cloud was just first coming out.'

We are at a time of AI: Game On. The financial press is claiming it's the AI arms race.

If you are not working out what this new arms race will add or subtract to your business, look out. It will impact all areas of life, business and society.

It is hard to get an accurate view of the real number of staff working at OpenAI, the company that enabled the ChatGPT-3 generative work. LinkedIn in March 2023 showed about 570 people. Think about that from a productivity perspective. Fewer than 1,000 people have built a tool that is changing the

---

3   Microsoft head of strategy in 1997.

world at a speed like nothing before. Now it may prove to be a moment in time; however, its impact will be long-lasting in terms of what it has done to the business world and the public's imagination of AI. IP and data outpacing labour and capital is evident in many areas and will grow from here.

For example, the cross-sell algorithm of Amazon generates approximately 35% of all Amazon retail sales. That is, when you buy a book, guitar or anything on Amazon, and the site responds with 'People who bought this book also bought …', that recommendation, which automatically and continuously adjusts in response to ongoing customer choices, drives an incredible volume of new sales. In dollar terms Amazon generates $48 billion from this algorithm.[4]

So, it could be argued that Amazon-held IP about customers and its algorithm is now worth more than almost every retailer on the planet, with the exception of giants like Walmart. IP and data are replacing labour and capital as the cornerstone of value creation and directors and executives need to be aware and forearmed about how they take their companies into the AI: Game On age.

While talking to a leading investment banker in the US, his thesis is to short companies that sell anything with a barcode. When he interviews CEOs of big retail companies, if their products are sold with a barcode, he asks, 'How do you plan to stop Amazon from selling that better and cheaper and with faster delivery than you?' If their answer is unsatisfactory, he puts in place share deals that bet on the decline of their stock. He was flabbergasted that so many CEOs rarely have a satisfactory answer. 'They give me some fluff about customer-centric initiatives, but most have not acted in a scaled way to put data and AI at the heart and spine of the company.' The boards of these organisations are in this right now and directors and executives need to make the organisation own its purpose, its ethics and the connection between its data-enabled spine, ethically based heart and all stakeholders. Lose the heart and you are a data-enabled AI pariah waiting for your media firestorm. Do too little and you are Kodak meets Blockbuster. Bed Bath & Beyond is a great case study. I know someone who worked in their analytics team in 2017. He became frustrated as the team leaders were too sure they had it all covered, claiming all this AI use, personalisation optimisation and more. Trouble was no one told the customers. A PowerPoint deck claiming you have this covered will not fly.

'Everybody knows that the guy with the best data on their customers' needs will win.' These words were said to me in a meeting in 1997 in Seattle at Microsoft head office. The executive was trying to work out how to capture the signals from millions of customers using his product so he could design a better product for them. The internet was still largely dial-up, slow and clunky.

---

4   https://www.envisionhorizons.com/blog/cross-selling-and-using-purchase-combinations-on-amazon.

Data strategy was not something you heard about in 1997 but these words stuck in my mind as the beginning of something significant.

Imagine trying to learn, in real time, what 200 million plus people were doing with your product in 1997. Back then it was like saying you were working on time travel. This approach, then so unique, has proved to be true and essential for survival. Yet many organisations nearly three decades later are still working on how to find their data strategy from real scaled customer insights. How is your organisation diversifying from commoditised legacy products that will be challenged in the future by data AI-enabled competitors? That is what boards and executives need to be asking.

The recent incredible advancements in AI will accelerate the advantages of companies that have powerful proprietary data sets. One of the world's most notorious stock pickers Cathie Wood, claimed in February 2023, 'We believe that the hidden gems that will benefit the most from artificial intelligence are those companies with proprietary datasets.' They claimed Tesla as a good example due to its data on roads and driving behaviours. Note, this is not investment advice!

The a16z podcast in January 2023 asked some of the Andreessen Horowitz investment partners for their themes on 2023. They said, 'If a company doesn't have an AI strategy, it should really be thinking about one yesterday.' The podcast made the point that they see lots of 10–100x productivity in organisations' back of house with AI. Procurement, finance and other areas, not just on the customer side. As AI use becomes table stakes you will need your own strategy to harness its power.

To not ask and act on these sorts of questions is going to limit your business as we enter the AI: Game On world.

Take the San Pellegrino I am drinking while writing this. Anyone can type it into Google, add 'lowest price' to their search and it will find the best offer as defined by Google SEO and paid ads. Strategy guru Michael Porter said, 'Business needs to decide to be cheap or different'; pain comes from an undifferentiated offering. We are now seeing different combined with cheaper. The low price – fast delivery offerings of giants such as Amazon are hard to beat, and customers will migrate when economic benefits accrue to them, especially from a trusted provider that removes friction from the purchase.

What does San Pellegrino know about its customers? It knows how many bottles in which sizes and flavours are made and sold in which regions by which retailers, but what can the company know about its customers' habits, where they drink San Pellegrino, for what purpose outside of thirst? Unless they augment their own warehouse data they will not know what customers eat when they're drinking it, how old they are, whether they're loyal or switch with the alternative sparkling waters, how price sensitive they are, or how much they typically consume each day. Nor what impact a SodaStream in their kitchen would have on that home's consumption. Is San Pellegrino mainly consumed just when entertaining? Such specific consumer insight from real data relies on the producer having a relationship with each customer, a direct line of sight to the customer via externally associated data. Supermarket loyalty cards were developed for this reason and do a good job if accompanied by great software and analytics.

That's why, if your business has very little interaction with or 'signal' from your customers, you should be alarmed and start devoting thought and resources to answering questions such as: How do I create signals directly with my customers? What products could I invent that will allow my customers to interact with me in a way that will increase customer signals, and what benefits can I provide to my customers from this signal? Make sure you answer this last question or you will be creating customer annoyance, not benefit. We are all inundated with apps, logins and loyalty programs all too often with nebulous value to us.

One global company supplying gas cylinders is looking at tackling this question. With millions of gas cylinders sent out to millions of customers, they currently don't know which gas cylinders are full or about to run empty. They're investigating what it would cost to put a tiny sensor and processor in each cylinder that would tell them where the bottle is and how full it is – it might be at a remote cattle station and maybe it's only 20% full. With that direct signal from the customer, the company can now create a service around how to replenish the gas. The customer could then get a message, 'Your gas bottle is about to run out, click here for a refill.' There are of course some ways of knowing how much gas is left with new tech, but there is, to my knowledge, no current holistic global feedback loop at scale.

This sort of initiative is useful for the customer because they're never caught short when they want to heat, cook or use gas for a variety of purposes. For the gas company it builds loyalty, tracks and predicts demand and data on which to potentially base other product offerings; it allows them to legitimately communicate with the customer in a value exchange that works for both.

The use of data and applied analytics is creating winners and losers in all aspects of business. A corporate Pearl Harbor awaits organisations not able to enable and decipher customer signals.

OLD V NEW STATE

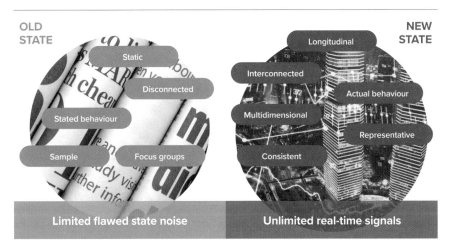

OLD STATE — Static · Disconnected · Stated behaviour · Sample · Focus groups — Limited flawed state noise

NEW STATE — Longitudinal · Interconnected · Actual behaviour · Multidimensional · Representative · Consistent — Unlimited real-time signals

Costs of not using data – the importance of observing and understanding

The surprise attack on Pearl Harbor stands out as one of the most catalytic moments in understanding the value of data. In early 1941 the US military was aware of the tensions with Japan, and a small team was working to crack the Japanese naval codes. Compared to amassing firepower and hardware, codebreaking was not a priority for military investment in those days.

Japan's raid on Pearl Harbor sharply illustrated that identifying and understanding a signal from noise that is outside the organisation, in this case cracking the codes of Japanese communications, was every bit as important as having aircraft carriers. The attack changed the US military's appreciation of data; the navy consequently invested heavily in mathematicians, codebreakers and information detection and developed a cohesive program that became mission-critical to winning the war.

Within a few months of Pearl Harbor the US military cracked the code of the Japanese and in turn knew that the Japanese invasion force, including many of the very aircraft carriers that had facilitated the attack on Pearl Harbor, were en route to the Midway Islands. This was achieved through finding the signal in the scrambled code of the communication of the Japanese military data – it enabled the US to decisively defeat Japan at the Battle of Midway, and this was the turning point in the war in the Pacific.

Pearl Harbor was, literally, a burning platform, and it drove decisive change through tragic loss. At some point, every business will face its own metaphorical

Pearl Harbor moment in that it will be surprised by competition often from outside its traditional frame of reference in a way it is unable to predict, that is unless they become an organisation with real predictive capabilities.

In business it is now imperative to understand and try to predict wherever possible macroeconomic changes, and micro-behavioural changes of the customer and marketplace in real time. If the US Navy had even one hour's notice of Pearl Harbor the result would have been very different.

One super-smart venture capitalist in Silicon Valley said something to me that still sticks in my mind. He said, 'If the company wants the consumer to sign a long-term contract, its customer service is most likely terrible. The contract is for their benefit not yours. It is to stop you leaving.' It made me realise that many of the highest-ranking companies for customer experience – Netflix, Google, Amazon, Alibaba, Apple – have no need for lock-in, long-term contracts (although most have subscription/premium offers and linked offers and services: Amazon Prime, Echo/Alexa, Google Nest, Apple's Siri). All these companies know their customers' actions at a moment in time and over time. It means they can more accurately predict the future needs of their customers. Compare this to most telecommunications companies, or many financial companies that sell multi-year contracts as it's often to their advantage not yours.

Ironically a range of these long-term telco contracts are for the leasing of Apple products. The world's most successful consumer company, Apple, does not need to contract us to a term, as we queue up for their new releases. Many telcos with mediocre service want a two-year term with penalties to give us access.

Companies mistake the loyalty of customers with a lack of options for customers to leave. And, when someone else understands their needs better than you, they move and you have no understanding of why. This is because the early signals in the data were missed, just like Pearl Harbor. Eventually the failure to act to understand the customer has a cost. It snowballs to the point that your effort to make your organisation more data-driven and more attractive becomes increasingly difficult.

From data-driven to AI-powered – the future of predictive companies

For decades some entrepreneurs, company executives and board members have recognised the importance of particular data sets and harnessed them. We're all familiar with the rise of the FAANGs (Facebook, Amazon, Apple, Netflix, Google), probably GAFAM (Google, Apple, Facebook, Amazon,

Microsoft)[5] and BATX (Baidu, Alibaba, Tencent, Xiaomi) – the data-driven giant companies.

Writing this in 2023, there have been some significant changes in value to the FAANG stocks; even with large-scale corrections they still have amassed massive valuations via their innovation from data use, and in some cases abuse. Not convinced? Look at the following two snapshots from a real-time link of the most valuable companies.

20 MOST VALUABLE FORTUNE 500 COMPANIES 1995–2023

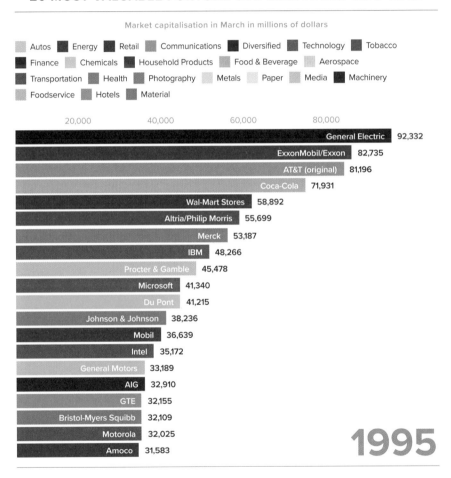

Market capitalisation in March in millions of dollars

Autos   Energy   Retail   Communications   Diversified   Technology   Tobacco
Finance   Chemicals   Household Products   Food & Beverage   Aerospace
Transportation   Health   Photography   Metals   Paper   Media   Machinery
Foodservice   Hotels   Material

General Electric	92,332
ExxonMobil/Exxon	82,735
AT&T (original)	81,196
Coca-Cola	71,931
Wal-Mart Stores	58,892
Altria/Philip Morris	55,699
Merck	53,187
IBM	48,266
Procter & Gamble	45,478
Microsoft	41,340
Du Pont	41,215
Johnson & Johnson	38,236
Mobil	36,639
Intel	35,172
General Motors	33,189
AIG	32,910
GTE	32,155
Bristol-Myers Squibb	32,109
Motorola	32,025
Amoco	31,583

1995

---

5   Given recent name changes a new acronym has been coined by Jim Cramer, MAMAA (Meta, Apple, Microsoft, Amazon, Alphabet).

20 MOST VALUABLE FORTUNE 500 COMPANIES 1995–2023

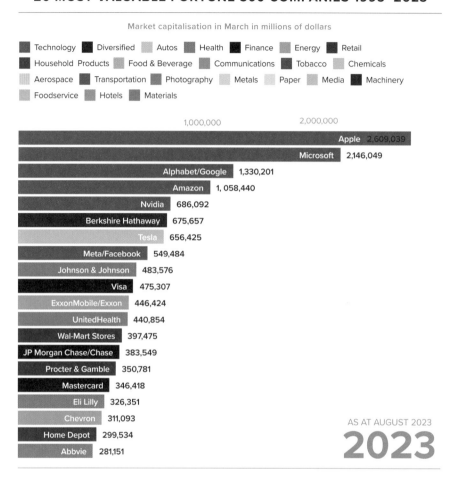

Market capitalisation in March in millions of dollars

Technology · Diversified · Autos · Health · Finance · Energy · Retail · Household Products · Food & Beverage · Communications · Tobacco · Chemicals · Aerospace · Transportation · Photography · Metals · Paper · Media · Machinery · Foodservice · Hotels · Materials

Company	Market capitalisation
Apple	2,609,039
Microsoft	2,146,049
Alphabet/Google	1,330,201
Amazon	1,058,440
Nvidia	686,092
Berkshire Hathaway	675,657
Tesla	656,425
Meta/Facebook	549,484
Johnson & Johnson	483,576
Visa	475,307
ExxonMobile/Exxon	446,424
UnitedHealth	440,854
Wal-Mart Stores	397,475
JP Morgan Chase/Chase	383,549
Procter & Gamble	350,781
Mastercard	346,418
Eli Lilly	326,351
Chevron	311,093
Home Depot	299,534
Abbvie	281,151

AS AT AUGUST 2023

2023

According to Boston Consulting Group (BCG) research from 2020, one in three public companies will cease to exist in its current form by 2025 – a rate six times higher than it was 40 years ago. Forty-four per cent of today's leading companies have only held their position for at least five years, down from 77% in 1970.[6]

In January 2021 Juniper, an AI engineering company, ran a survey of 700 organisations across multiple sectors from agribusiness, industrial, tech, pharma and across Asia, Europe and North America.[7] The survey included

6   https://www.bcg.com/en-us/featured-insights/how-to/thrive-in-the-2020s.

7   https://www.juniper.net/content/dam/www/assets/additional-resources/us/en/juniper-ai-research-paper.pdf.

large, capitalised companies greater than $5 billion down to small businesses with sub $50 million revenues. The research noted that the top three challenges for companies were AI-ready technology stacks, workforce readiness and AI governance.

It also found 95% of organisations believe they would benefit from embedding AI into their daily operations, products and services, yet only 6% of C-suite level leaders reported AI-powered solutions across their organisation. Even the most advanced companies with AI can still find a myriad of new ways to use this technology.

In 2023 McKinsey & Company research found that 90% of commercial leaders expect to utilise AI solutions often in the next two years.

There are some logical steps you can take to change the way your company approaches becoming an AI/data-driven business. The first step is to understand where your company is now, what's coming next from this frontier in terms of data and the customer, the flow of data (or not) across the organisation (and up and down the decision chain). This will give you a baseline of where to start. Then you need to build a road map (or should I say data map and strategy) that includes options and how to 'do no harm' (trust, privacy and value exchange).

It's no coincidence that many of the wealthiest people in the world at the time of writing are founders of data-rich companies where the value creation is attributed to data-driven enterprises: Elon Musk, Jeff Bezos, Mark Zuckerberg, Larry Page, Sergey Brin among others. There is, of course, some very real concern about the concentration of this power, and in some of the use cases along with the way data is stored and used. We will look at some of this later in the book.

So why are so many companies so slow off the mark to immerse themselves in data and AI to ensure future business performance and success?

Churchill purportedly said, 'Success is going from failure to failure without loss of enthusiasm.' This, I know, could be a description of many customer transformation/digital transformation programs over the past 20 years, most of which fail as they have been driven too much from a technology fix, and too little around the business needs, business adaptation and customer fit. Too much of a digital veneer (usually in the customer experience/interface area), and too little appreciation that it's a whole-of-business project, and that it never stops.

CHAPTER TAKEAWAYS

1. Data and AI are the drivers of future economic growth and value, replacing labour and capital as the cornerstone of value creation.

2. Companies that embrace AI and data are outperforming those that don't have a cohesive response to AI.

3. Companies that know their customers' signals and behaviour can more accurately predict future needs and stay competitive by make barriers to entry higher.

4. The top three challenges for companies are AI-ready technology stacks, workforce readiness and AI governance.

5. While most organisations believe they would benefit from AI, only 6% of C-level leaders reported AI-powered solutions across their organisation.

Chapter 2

THE DATA AND AI BUCK STOPS WITH THE BOARD

'It's not what we don't know that gets us in trouble.
It's what we know for sure that just ain't so.' – Mark Twain

Boards and executives are now responsible for the poor use of data

BrisConnections was a consortium of three companies (Macquarie Bank, Thiess and John Holland) that were awarded the public-private partnership contract for the Airport Link, a motorway-grade toll road in the northern suburbs of Brisbane. BrisConnections commissioned its engineering partner, Arup, to investigate the prospects for an Airport Link tunnel, a 6.7-km toll road that connects the Brisbane CBD with the Clem Jones Tunnel and the arterial road leading to Brisbane Airport.

Within seven months from the opening of the major toll road, in July 2012, BrisConnections went into administration causing the loss of billions. The cause? Actual traffic turned out to be dramatically below the forecast flow. The prediction of customers' intention was a complete failure.

In the litigation that followed the directors found out that use of data matters to the tune of a $2 billion class action that was launched. Under the scrutiny of the court process the forecaster conceded the models used to forecast the use of the road was 'utterly absurd', leaving a multibillion-dollar hole.

The BrisConnections litigation opened the whole debate about whether data was too important to be left to the data department. The answer was clearly yes. It wasn't just the professional firms that were held to account, it was board members. The lesson? Boards and management need to get much better at real data diligence, and ask questions such as: What data goes into the model? Where did it come from? What biases could be in it? What is our comfort score on how accurate this is? Can it be independently verified? What other sources of data could add to our analysis?

We are all afflicted by confirmation bias. We want our beliefs confirmed. Information that supports confirmation bias can trigger a dopamine release that makes it very comforting. Being wrong is dopamine-depleting and all people avoid this feeling, even when it is good for them. Advice that is counter to our own opinions is often rejected.

Infrastructure and the use of data have been around us for millennia. Consider Dr John Snow. Conventional wisdom during the cholera pandemic in London in 1854 was that it was an airborne disease, the logic being that the smell of sewerage was all over London, as the sewer system was being built and many people were dying of this terrible disease. One lone voice, Dr John Snow, said he thought the disease was in London's drinking water. He was ridiculed and then he created a map of the deaths. It showed that the closer you lived to one particular water pump the more likely it was that you would die. Once the data was plotted and visualised, it was understood by humans – and it paved the path to the end of that sad chapter in London's history. Data hunts and kills myths, provided you have an open mind to the new data.

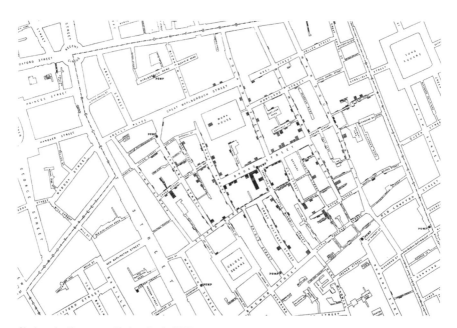

Cholera deaths mapped in London in 1854

BrisConnections was the first time I can remember an Australian board being sued for poor use of data, for not taking reasonable care to assess the data it had commissioned. The already long, costly and multi-pronged litigation continued through to 2017.[8][9] Boards and senior executives now need to 'own' the data they use for AI-enabled predictions of future adoption and use cases.[10]

This failure is a lesson for all directors, executives and professionals for many reasons. It makes clear that the predictions you make from the data you use or don't use are auditable. What you did with it can be audited, and also what you did not do with it. It shows that, as expectations increase and better data sets become available, the idea that a small survey sample size can be used to justify huge investment decisions is not going to fly. In court you'll sit in front of a judge, and expert witnesses, people like me, will say, 'You could have predicted demand for the Airport Link more precisely if you'd used contemporary data science and external data sets and analytics. You can now build an AI-predictive model of every car owner and their unique propensity to use that toll road.' This could be done in a privacy-compliant manner with de-identified data sets.

In today's world of predictive analytics of real-world data enabling AI, it is possible to build a toll road that is targeted at specific societal needs. First, identify the problem to be solved. Say it's to improve the speed and convenience of access from the CBD and catchment areas en route to the airport or other destinations along the road. Then, look at the proposal through the lens of the customer. Who is the customer? Where is the customer? Where are they going? Why are they going? What alternative modes of travel do they have? What public transport options could be considered? What second-order impacts are there in the local area: noise, pollution, endangered species and more?

Those questions might lead to the commissioning of data on car ownership in the area served, common destinations or routes driven, and the population's financial capacity to pay the toll. The linkages with plans for public transport in the area and the viable alternatives to using a toll road need to be factored in.

If another operator is opening a light rail right beside the road, for example, it could have a huge impact on traffic projections as will the growth of ridesharing, and ultimately autonomous vehicles. Also, if you are contemplating a project with the life of a toll road, you should consider future developments like drones

8   https://www.globalconstructionreview.com/arup-settles-australian-lawsuit-over-utterly-absur/.

9   http://www.afr.com/brand/rear-window/arup-macquarie-and-brisconnections-let-the-tunnel-wars-begin-20170420-gvodph.

10   https://www.globalconstructionreview.com/arup-settles-australian-lawsuit-over-utterly-absur/
     http://www.afr.com/brand/rear-window/arup-macquarie-and-brisconnections-let-the-tunnel-wars-begin-20170420-gvodph.

or similar technology that can transport people, as well as other possible road transport substitutes. Then there is trend data. How many young people are in the catchment area? And what is their propensity to learn to drive and to buy a car? What are the trends for people working from home, or hybrid work involving only one or more days a week in the office, as well as trends around teleconferencing and the advent of telepresence robots?

Such factors are predictive of traffic flows, so too is telco data showing mobile phone usage in areas, as are other location data from apps, Uber trips and the like. These data sets make the assumptions of BrisConnections (and others like it) look like a horse-drawn cart compared to the latest Mars rover.

DIVERSE DATA ALLOWS LEADERS TO ASK BETTER GOVERNANCE QUESTIONS

| Where to invest capital? | Which customers are price elastic? | Which customers will defect? | What will they buy next? |
| Blip or revenue cliff coming? | Did marketing work? | Competitor impacts | What is the next best customer conversation? |

As you can see in the graphic above, quality data sheds light on the micro and the macro; it gives us both telescopic and microscopic perspectives.

We've seen that to underinvest in how to answer such questions, or to be incapable of reading the anomalies in questionable data, can be seen as bordering on negligence in today's data-driven world.

Coca-Cola disastrously changed their formula in 1995 to New Coke after customer research said consumers preferred the new taste. The focus groups misled them, and it was a near-death experience for the company. They changed the formula back to the original Coke as they concluded through sales falling fast that 'marketing was too important to be left to the marketing department'.

I have seen many cases where data has become too important to be left to the data department, as is evidenced by the litigation in relation to BrisConnections.

Data use, and misuse, is a whole-of-organisation strategic issue. You may well have and/or need a great data department, but it has to be fully integrated within your organisation, not an island of mathematical rigour and data science. Amazon does not have a data business. It has a customer business fed and increasingly led by customer data.

AI and data-led companies require a different kind of leadership and governance

In Nancy Giordano's book *Leadering*, she delves into the future of company stewardship. The gist of her message is that there has to be a transition from leadership to leadering, from 'a static, closed, hierarchical, organisational approach designed to scale efficiently for consistent, short-term growth, to leadership that cultivates a dynamic, adaptive, caring, inclusive mindset which supports continuous innovation for long-term, sustainable value.'[11]

Using this model of 'leadering', it becomes easier to achieve what needs to be done to plan and execute data and AI utilisation, as it should be led from the top down. The board and executives can lead this change:

- **Devising a plan for how AI will benefit the organisation, its staff, customers and society**

  It's critical to have a vision for how AI will impact your business over the next three years. What does good look like? How can data help the strategy or enlighten the strategy? What are the risks of using data compared to the risks of not using data? What use cases would drive material, positive change? Recent BCG-MIT research found that companies with the right data, technology and talent, but with no clear strategy, only have a 21% chance of achieving significant benefits.

- **Allowing disparate teams to work together**

  A company that wants to succeed with AI needs to thoughtfully remove barriers to information use that empower teams to explore new ways of working together. This will help improve agility and innovation and takes the organisation to a more holistic view of the customer, the market and the opportunities.

- **Leaning into diversity**

  Diversity of thought is key to a data strategy, so make sure teams have diverse perspectives across data and AI applications.

---

11   https://leadering.us/.

- **Rethinking how people interact with machines (and vice versa)**

  BCG research shows that when you create feedback loops in AI deployment, there's a greater chance of success. To seize on this, you'll want AI learning from human feedback, humans learning from AI, and AI learning autonomously. Then repeat the cycle.

Changing your business to be data-driven with AI doesn't just require a change in technology, it demands a change in process, culture and collaboration. One CEO who is on this path, and doing it well, said to me that for every dollar they spend on tech and data, they spend one on change management initiatives. He claimed this was the secret to their data innovation.

AI/data versus human decision-making

If you're a professional lawyer, accountant, engineer or doctor, your position is most likely already changing in significant ways due to data and AI. This change is now in every aspect of our lives: education, health, housing, recreation, our cities, the environment, investments and who we elect. Even our laws and how our justice system operates have components of data and AI in them. The recent advances in OpenAI's ChatGPT and other large-scale language models are showing profound advancements in AI use cases. Some are very good, some alarmingly bad. A friend of mine ran multiple experiments on several of the new AI-enabled systems to find information about Paul Graham, a founder of Y Combinator. The text was thoroughly convincing, yet completely wrong. My friend went on to say that OpenAI and ChatGPT appear prone to favour text written by other AI over human writing.

Just think about that for a moment.

We could be at the place where we down-rank human thought and up-rank AI because of our own bias to find the machine's writing more plausible! In Chapter 6 I will share the story about judges and the pattern of their decision-making before and after breaks and lunch. The point is machines have biases and so do humans.

Data and AI already affect our political system. In Australia the only exemption for the use of private information in marketing and direct mail is for political parties. They can access the electoral roll and write to you directly. This information is, rightly, off limits for all other uses and perhaps it should be off limits to political parties too. Millions of Australians have received texts from political parties that we have never opted into. The results of each election are pored over by political strategists of all parties, and the detail in the data would surprise many. The Census collector district (approximately 200 homes) in Australia that is the most marginal is knowable. Who the people in those 200 or more homes are is also knowable. What would make them change their vote? That is predictable, and what policy ideas will resonate with them is also predictable if enough data is brought to the table, or more accurately, to the machines.

If you're like me and have wondered why on earth a new government policy is introduced when it seems counter to common sense, it could well be that the answer lies in the data the politicians are reviewing. The trouble for society here is that data use of this nature is optimised for swinging voters in marginal electorates and that is not always to the benefit of our wider society.

Data and AI are changing and will continue to change every aspect of our lives. This is on top of many other profound transformations. We've just been living through one of the most challenging periods of the last 50 years. We have had a one-in-100-year global pandemic, followed by massive trade instability as a result of Russia's war on Ukraine, and we are experiencing the influence of climate change. All of which have resulted in significant disruption. Resilience and adaptive capabilities may have never been more important than they are today, for individuals, organisations and societies.

The capturing, harnessing and sharing of data and its interpretation has, arguably, enabled the world's leaders and medical professionals to research, develop and deliver pandemic responses vastly more effectively and efficiently than we've ever seen before. This has saved millions of lives, reducing the impact of the virus on millions of others and averting a global economic crisis.

AI is being deployed across a wide range of health and medical treatments. For example, take the assessment of lung cancer from X-rays. One doctor/radiologist can only look at a certain number of X-rays per day and use their knowledge to look for health problems like cancer. An AI machine capable of continually learning can view thousands per day. Combine the radiologist with the machine and you've now got significantly increased capability. There is real excitement about how AI can notice correlations and early signs of other diseases. Some of this has not been picked up before and is now being investigated further by humans.

I recently saw a demonstration of Enlitic.com in a public forum, which was impressive, showing the scanning of thousands of X-rays to detect anomalies at incredible speed and great accuracy. They are focused on solutions using AI tools that positively impact patient care and that their AI can find health issues with greater accuracy than doctors alone and at much greater speeds.[12] They stress that this system needs to be used in tandem with doctors and it is in no way a replacement of doctors. Rather, the technology allows the doctor to spend more of their time focused on high-value tasks including more dialogue with patients.

---

12   https://www.enlitic.com/.

For the financial sector, especially in Australia, the Royal Commission into Misconduct in the Banking, Superannuation and Financial Services Industry, and resultant responsible lending recommendations, has effectively changed the law in terms of home loans. It's moved from 'let the buyer beware' to 'let the seller beware'. Banks and other financial institutions around the world are going to need specific criteria to decide which products they can sell to who. If you are not using real data to know your customer and what you could or should not be selling to them, a regulator may well want to ask you why not?

While Know Your Customer (KYC) is something that banks are regulated to comply with – mainly for anti-money laundering purposes – they, and other large companies, are all aiming at some form of customer-centric goal. The reality is AI is not being deployed at anywhere near the scale and sophistication to really know their customers, or better still predict what they need, when they need it.

Here's a recent personal example. I received a cheque. Do you remember them? So, I found the bank branch and deposited the cheque, and, as I did so, the teller asked me if I needed a car loan. I felt sorry for the teller, because I'd paid cash for my car with that bank, so my transaction history inside of the bank tells them I don't need a car loan, but the teller at the front desk didn't have that information. Rather he had a self-serving instruction from head office to try and sell car loans. My data is there to be used for my benefit, but their systems are too disconnected to empower the teller with the next best conversation to have with me for my benefit. Banks with better management focused on customer innovation with data, and fintech challengers, will not be this slow to use their customers' data and will be able to create the next best action – a conversation with the customer, based on their specific needs.

It's hard when you're the incumbent because ego and hubris get in the way. In his 2014 letter to Berkshire Hathaway shareholders Warren Buffett referred to his ABC checklist:

> 'My successor will need one other particular strength: the ability to fight off the ABCs of business decay, which are arrogance, bureaucracy and complacency. When these corporate cancers metastasize, even the strongest of companies can falter.'[13]

---

13 https://markets.businessinsider.com/news/stocks/warren-buffett-bill-melinda-gates-foundation-ceo-abcs-philanthropy-dangers-2021-7.

Data AI capability/data AI leadership scarcity

Several years ago, the challenge for business was that they didn't have enough accessible data. The start of the typical data journey is that data is in different formats, in different parts of the business, and is not shared. In many cases, data is actively hidden or held back from other parts of the business. Knowledge is power; pay and advancement have, up until now, been tied to data silos, making knowledge a power paradox.

Most digital transformation projects are specific, time-limited projects, rather than an integrated, whole-of-business transformation that puts data at the centre of everything. In Chapter 5, I explore the data spine concept, and how successful companies today and tomorrow will have a data spine that supports the flow of data throughout the organisation, and it's this approach that is a true data transformation.

The real scarcity for businesses now is in identifying or developing leaders, executives, board members and founders who are able to recreate their companies or build new ventures that can find and use data and AI to deliver a new sort of customer advantage.

The data-driven giants, like Amazon, Apple, Netflix, Alphabet, Microsoft, Tesla and Meta, are using data and AI to create advantage. Some will also know about other interesting companies such as Adobe, Klarna, Reonomy, FourKites, Databricks, Canva, Teradata IBM and Cloudera.[14] The list of companies and organisations that are yet to make data a core part of their strategic orientation is much longer.

In 2022, McKinsey examined the one constant throughout the data era: the need to learn, adapt and change. They also noted that when change accelerates so does the need to learn. If that's the case, then is there any place better to learn than from your customers' needs? The most powerful way to learn what your customers' needs are is through what they are sharing with you in a privacy-compliant and respectful way.

An organisation's ability to learn and rapidly translate that learning into action is the ultimate competitive advantage. This is where data analytics and AI thrive. The capabilities capture the signals of the customer in real time. They can respond in real time, and know who to alert in real time, if needed. They can also help predict future needs and wants, link up production, stock control, delivery and pricing, all in real time. This is a predictive business.

There are now companies that create algorithms at speed, with some claiming to create 200,000 algorithms a day. One such company, DataRobot, in 2021

---

14   https://builtin.com/big-data/big-data-companies-roundup.

was valued at $6.3 billion.[15] Interestingly, they refer to augmented intelligence, not artificial intelligence. Augmented intelligence is focused on how the software, data sets and technology can help humans make decisions. AI by contrast, in its purest sense, is software data sets and technology that will make its own decisions. The augmented decision is prompting the human, just as your maps do when driving and the map shows you a new option to save time. The AI reads the text and will make a summary; it has decided what was important in the text and gave the answer based on its programming determinants.

When Marc Andreessen said 'software is eating the world' in 2011, even he could not see that in 2023 AI will eat software, as claimed by Sarah Wang in a recent podcast.[16]

Self-adapting algorithms (SAMs) have been around for some time and now it is common for code to write code. In February 2023, Microsoft claims more than 100 million software developers are now using GitHub Copilot. The type of tasks you aim that code at, and for what purpose, is increasingly going to decide your corporate outcomes and reputational risks. It ends up ultimately as a board responsibility, because it if goes wrong the directors will own the downside, perhaps more than they might own the upside. Increasingly, the destiny of the organisation will be tied to code, how this fulfils the organisation's mission, its purpose, and how that all aligns with society's expectations. It is hard to imagine for some, but it is the new reality.

In visiting Microsoft in May 2023, it was interesting to see how they are adding the Copilot concept to many of their products. For example, they are developing new ways to summarise hundreds of emails and prepare the best responses in draft, or the reading of spreadsheets with automated insights. Or, how about summaries of Teams meetings with automated allocation of tasks and outcomes prepared for the host of the meeting.

These tools and more will speed up the adoption of AI-enabled tools, and the democratisation of these tools, to hundreds of millions of users.

The frontier of the cloud wars of Azure, Amazon, Google and others is now focused on smart AI cloud services. The cloud with the smartest tools will take share from the clouds without the tools. This is going to see much faster adoption of AI tools in all aspects of human endeavour.

---

15   https://www.reuters.com/technology/ai-tech-firm-datarobot-valued-63-bln-after-300-mln-investment-2021-07-27/#:~:text=AI%20tech%20firm%20DataRobot%20valued%20at%20%246.3%20bln%20after%20%24300%20mln%20investment,-Reuters.

16   Sarah Wang, general partner on the Growth investing team at Andreessen Horowitz, a16z podcast, Jan 2023.

It is the acceleration of the brave new world now, the world that Kevin Kelly describes as one of data flows, cognifying, screening, accessing, sharing and filtering.

An a16z podcast, on 17 February 2023, titled '1000x Developer' contained an interview with the CEO of Replit, a company that is focused on using AI to help developers. The CEO was talking about a future where there could be 1,000x uplift in productivity for developers. He made the point that in approximate numbers, only around 1% of people can code. The demand for new code is off the charts, and AI-driven tools that nudge the code writers with better and faster options are what Replit aims to do.

I am unsure whether this is good or bad technology, only observing that if your technology could get even a 2x uplift with new tools you would want to be exploring that. The Replit CEO went on to talk about bounty hunters of new code and creating tools like 99 Designs for code creation, enabled with new AI tools.

What's your role as an executive or board member in the AI: Game On world?

It is worth reflecting on some questions at this point.

1. What is the role of CEO in a world where the machines are outperforming people, repeatedly, in the ability to find and process information?

2. What is the role of the board in their fiducial responsibility for such a system of machines?

3. What are the regulatory issues here and how does the board and society mitigate risk in such a world?

There is probably a book in each of these, and I will certainly explore more and share some thoughts in other chapters. The most important actions you can take as an executive or board member right now are to:

1. Govern for our time

Governance is from the Latin word *gubernare* meaning 'to steer'. The better the data, the better the capacity to create insights and actions to control the course of the organisation. If you embrace data, AI and machine learning across your whole organisation and build your business with an enterprise-wide privacy-compliant data spine, you are on your way to the first version of your own AI: Game On business.

2. Understand and embrace machine learning

The next step, one that is already being implemented in organisations around the world, is the evolution of the 'machine learning machine'.

This is the predictive company of tomorrow, when data, AI and machine learning combine with a human team who learn to integrate machine learning and AI into their decision-making capability.

These are two profound responsibilities, and they cannot be avoided if your organisation hopes to be around for tomorrow.

I was lucky enough to see Garry Kasparov talk at South by Southwest (SXSW) in 2019. Kasparov became the youngest ever undisputed World Chess Champion in 1985 at age 22. In 1997 he became the first world champion to lose a match to a computer, under standard time controls, when he lost to the IBM supercomputer Deep Blue.[17]

Garry shared what it was like to lose to a machine, something not many of us had confronted, back in 1997. Garry was in no way worried about it. In fact, he said that since then, chess has become a game of humans and machines. It is the augmentation of human and machines, not replacement of humans. These chess masters had to decide who or what decides decades ago. When do you allow the machine to make the move and when do you not is now a decision for all leaders.

CEOs and boards are already making decisions augmented with machines and data, perhaps not in the way that Marc Benioff, CEO of Salesforce, Jeff Bezos, founder of Amazon, and Satya Nadella, CEO of Microsoft, are doing. Nonetheless, data, AI and machine learning are the next levels of being able to delve into, view and act on the data your organisation is creating every second of every day and, at times, adding in other data sets to refine your data. What is new is the quantum of information, the potential flow from customer needs from data observed to the boardroom and back; it's like a backbone of data (with spinal fluid) when it's built and integrated correctly.

Ask questions about the customer and keep asking questions

Make sure you learn whatever it is you can learn about your customers. To quote Jack Welch, whose legacy is clearly complex:

> **'There's only two ways to win. Work out what your customer wants and do it faster than anyone else.'**

To build a truly customer-centric company you need to lead this as a whole-of-organisation challenge.

---

17   https://en.wikipedia.org/wiki/Deep_Blue_(chess_computer).

Organisational design for a company with predictive capabilities starts from an appreciation that the data, AI and machine learning come from all over the company, and flow from bottom to top and back again. This is what Tesla has, Microsoft has, John Deere and a growing list of new and older companies have. Complete visibility in real time about what customers are buying, how they are using the products or services, the rate at which they are using or buying, the applications they're using and how often, how long they're taking, and so on. This information flows through to all parts of the business. To supply chains, warehousing, logistics, the sales team, to the product designers, developers, tech teams, call-centre support teams, sales and marketing teams, and not to be left out, to the executive and the board of directors.

The 'need to know' model of business has changed to the 'need to share'

The need to share is organisation-wide. The failure to connect the data across your business is costing your business now and it will cost it more in the future. The world had a tragic example of this failure in the 9/11 attacks in the USA. The failure of numerous government agencies, including the CIA, FBI, NSA, FAA and others, to connect the data and the dots resulted in a significant change in inter-agency sharing of data and intelligence to blend their databases for more comprehensive information analysis. The 9/11 Commission Report makes interesting reading, not least of all section 13.3 Unity of Effort in Sharing Information.[18]

Isolating data, AI and machine learning responsibility to one individual, your CDO or CIO, who then has to wrestle with the whole organisation, is not a way to scale data-driven customer-centricity. Organisational-wide leadership and management ownership, with KPIs anchored to the customer experience and return on customer experience, are needed.

Sharing data internally is now fraught with risk that this data can be shared externally via nefarious means. The risk of cyber theft cannot become the reason you get taken to the cleaners by competitors with better data and better AI-driven offerings for your customers. Navigating the cyber risk terrain means looking at the upside as well as the downside. If organisations can't imagine or see the upside, then all this talk about data and AI is just sitting on the risk register.

It is not about taking risks with cyber theft, open APIs, sloppy data hygiene, training or cyber security. It is about data safety and alignment with a use case that takes you to the future before your competitors find the upside.

---

18   https://www.9-11commission.gov/report/911Report.pdf.

It boils down to this: if you lock the data up, you lose; if you let the data rip, you lose.

That is why we need leaders who are thinking about what the AI: Game On future is all about. With real board engagement in the space, and thoughtful customer-centric use cases. Get help. Just like you would with any other issue as complex as AI and data. Data and AI can't be sugar-coated as easy to enable and win with in an ethical manner. Anyone who tells you it is easy is not doing it right.

Be curious and foster a culture that is curious. As Albert Einstein said, 'I have no special talents. I am only passionately curious.'

The late astronomer Carl Sagan said, 'Somewhere, something incredible is waiting to be known.' And that is a great way to start a data strategy.

THE TEAM WITH THE BEST DATA WIN

Information		
High information Low imagination	Unlimited information Unlimited imagination
Limited information Limited imagination	Low information High imagination
Imagination		

In the next chapter I'll delve into the ethics of data and AI, including who owns data, how companies can use it, and what you can do to protect it and share it if you want to. I'll also discuss AI and the pitfalls of waiting for regulation to catch up.

CHAPTER TAKEAWAYS

1. Data is too important to be left to the data department; boards and management need to inform themselves.

2. The failure of BrisConnections demonstrates the importance of auditable predictions using contemporary data science and analytics.

3. AI is transforming healthcare and finance, increasing capability and accuracy, and moving towards a customer-centric approach. Other sectors are following.

4. The Royal Commission into Misconduct in the Banking, Superannuation and Financial Services Industry resulted in changing the ethos to 'let the seller beware'.

5. An organisation's ability to learn and translate that learning into action is the ultimate competitive advantage, and data analytics and AI thrive in capturing signals of customer needs.

Chapter 3

THE IMPORTANCE OF TRUST

A letter from the Australian Institute of Company Directors (AIDC):

Dear Tim,

Today more than two thousand people were left disappointed when the stream failed for our LinkedIn Live launch of the new Cybersecurity Governance Principles.

We sincerely apologise to all of those in attendance.

This appears to have been a technical failure, and the experience was not consistent with the high standards you rightly expect from us. We are working with LinkedIn and our providers to understand this issue. A recording of the event is available below.

Malicious links

We also want to draw attention to suspected malicious links that may have been posted in the event chat during the 15 minutes before the event was cancelled.

- These links may have led to pages requesting personal information.
- These links were not posted by the AICD.
- If you clicked on such a link and entered your details, you should contact your financial institution. We would be grateful if you also let us know so that we can support where possible.
- If you did not, then you do not need to take any action.

There is no connection between the links that appeared on the LinkedIn platform and the AICD's data, which remains secure.

While it is possible that hackers targeted the event with malicious links, there is no known connection between those actions and the failure of the event to stream.

In response to this issue, we are working with the Australian Cyber Security Centre and LinkedIn to investigate the matter.

Cybersecurity Governance Principles

While no organisation is immune from cybersecurity risk, we are disappointed that the launch of the Cybersecurity Governance Principles was not able to be brought to you live.

We hope you find the principles themselves to be valuable in managing security threats, and that the recording below provides insight into applying the principles in your own context.

Some time ago I joined a director training session on cybercrime hosted by the Australian Institute of Company Directors (AICD). As you can see from the above letter, it didn't go so well, as it seemed the event was pulled because of malicious activity. The AICD works hard to help directors become more professional and informed. They were the victims of a cyberattack. The email above was sent out after the failed event. When this arrived my first thought was, 'Is this real or is this spam? Is it a real threat?'

The use and misuse of data is now the topic of the day in all boardrooms that care about where their business is going. The old adage 'Only two things in life are certain: death and taxes' needs an update. A friend of mine in Silicon Valley Ramneek Gupta, suggested a new version: 'The two things in life that are certain: death and a cyber breach.'

Boards should now be asking these sorts of questions.

- What data do we hold?
- Who has access and why?
- What parts of this data are mission-critical to our operation and what could we let go of?
- Why do we hold it, e.g. for a regulator, for our use, innovation, other?
- What benefit does the customer get from this?
- How is it encrypted?
- How is it protected?
- How is it backed up?
- Have we tested where the vulnerabilities are in our protection of the data?

The irony of most of the data crimes – ransom attacks and the like – is that the thieves are after personal information (PI): identity data, credit cards, medical records, passport numbers, Medicare numbers, even information about your employer and the like. Yet, in many of the most powerful use cases in analytics, the engines don't need PI to predict next best offers or to solve customer pain points. At the time of writing, Amazon's personalisation engine has not been hacked and it's the summary of billions of purchase patterns.

As cyberattacks increase in frequency and scale there is an increasing breakdown in trust between companies and their customers and the community. In 2022 alone, here in Australia, we have witnessed major cyberattacks on Optus, Medibank, the AFP, Vinomofo and others.[19] A recent McKinsey report notes that 85% of respondents said that knowing a company's data privacy policy was important before making a purchase. The trust of the customer in how your organisation stores and uses their data is critical.

In her illuminating book *Who Can You Trust?: How Technology Brought Us Together and Why It Might Drive Us Apart*,[20] Rachel Botsman explores the fragility of trust at all levels of society, especially corporations with a large power imbalance between them and their customers. Rachel was on the NRMA board for a few years, and they were very lucky to have her expertise. To summarise some of Rachel's work: trust is an enabler. Lose it and you have a big problem. As the world becomes more hostile with cybercrime, radicalism and fatigue, post-Covid businesses need to take significantly more care with their customers around trust. Customers are looking at what businesses do, or don't do, with their data; the value of the communication they are being provided with (and unsubscribing if it's of no value); and increasingly wanting a 'human option' when they need help.

The rapid trajectory of consumers adopting digital business offerings has been incredible. Think of the self-services via intuitive apps for the likes of Airbnb, Uber, Waze and Spotify.

The harder place to compete is in the hybrid area, which requires great digital capability and human care when needed. Apple does this brilliantly. You can do so much with them digitally. However, if you get to the point where you need real help, you can log a callback and a human being will call you at your convenience. I've used this option a couple of times myself for more complex issues and it illustrates why Apple is one of the true leaders in customer care. They also have retail stores with staff who are well equipped to help customers. Not surprisingly, this leads to loyalty and a massive gain in their market valuation. At the time of writing, Apple was the most valuable company on the planet.

---

19   https://www.webberinsurance.com.au/data-breaches-list.

20   https://www.amazon.com.au/Who-Can-You-Trust-Technology/dp/1541773675.

If your organisation pushes customers to chat rooms for help with bots that are substandard or artificially inept versus artificially intelligent, you are on a collision course to customer churn, short sellers and, quite possibly, your own Kodak moment. I have spent hours dealing with one of the makers of multimedia software who push the customer to bots on complex issues that are simply not able to be solved through a chat with a bot. The customer's pain point should be the moment of innovation, yet the signal is lost as they miss the pain of customers as the frustrated customer curses the bot. Eventually, you get handed off to what now feels like a human in the chat room. I feel for these staff, who are probably multitasking many customers at once, as you restate all the issues again and again. One phone call would likely solve most issues fast and give valuable insight into the customer's pain point, but the digital self-services-only mantra doesn't allow for this. Rather, it is more like artificial ineptitude than intelligence and it will put you on a collision course with reality. For some of these firms, the displeasure of the customer is being reflected in the share price. The board needs to own this and accept it is on them.

Boards and executives need to be clear on the unintended consequences of any new technology. Especially the extent to which it does or does not align with human beings and societal norms. This starts with purpose and making sure people are central in this process. As Satya Nadella, CEO of Microsoft, said, 'It starts, by the way, with design AI, you can have the human in the loop, you can have the human on the loop or you can have the human out of the loop.' He went on to say in February 2023, 'When you think about these generative AI models, remember one thing: they are prompted to do things. The prompting comes from a human being.' This may change in the future as some who fear where AI is heading point out.

Nadella makes the point that the pre-training is crucial. This is where the model is made safe, and what happens at this stage will matter a great deal in application contexts. Humans will still be responsible for deciding who or what decides.

A data AI Hippocratic oath

The Hippocratic oath is one of the oldest binding documents in history and is still held sacred by physicians: to treat the ill to the best of one's ability, to preserve a patient's privacy, to teach the secrets of medicine to the next generation.

Greg Schneider is co-founder of Quantium, and he was the first person I heard talk about a data Hippocratic oath. I think all businesses need a data Hippocratic oath. If you are looking for a North Star to aim your data and AI ethics at, and to abide by, here's a starting point:

1. We will do no harm with the data we collect.

2. We will not use the information about any human being for any purpose that makes that person's life harder.

3. We will respect the privacy of our customers, and not allow information on them to be used against them in any way.

Customers are concerned about their privacy, which most people regard as sacrosanct. This concern applies to what data a business collects, what it's used for now and into the future, how long it's kept for and what, if any, third parties you share it with. Organisations on their way to being a predictive organisation need to protect the data collected, stored and used. They must anticipate the future uses of the data they are collecting and only collect the data they really need to help customers. Moreover, they must enable its removal at the customer's request. If you don't undertake all these actions there may well be consequences – personal, financial, reputational and regulatory.

Data use and misuse

As data sets grow and data use cases expand so too do the possibilities for use and misuse. The need for data 'guard rails' can't be retrofitted after a data train crash. The guard rails don't need to be as large as *War and Peace*, but they do need to be clear, and a data Hippocratic oath is one framework that can help. This is where boards, senior executives and management need to go deep. If you don't know what the data is, how it was obtained, and what it will be used for, you may find yourself in front of a regulator or senate committee trying to explain it later. 'I left that to the data department' is not going to fly in a witness box. What was the data department doing? Did they have a data Hippocratic oath or other guard rails that they lived by? What second- or third-order consequences are there in the data use, or misuse? Is this on your risk register? Did the board bring an inquiring mind to this subject matter?

Governments need to move faster in relation to regulation, to stay in front of enforcement of data and AI use, and protecting the privacy of data from companies with poor ethical standards, as well as pursue the prosecution of criminals who illegally acquire data for commercial gain. Now that AI is growing at incredible speed, regulators will need to quickly form a view and take action regarding what is right for society.

In February 2022 Andrew Forrest, an Australian mining magnate and philanthropist, launched criminal proceedings against the Meta platform Facebook in an Australian court, alleging that it breached anti-money laundering laws, and its platform is used to scam.[21] Forrest said he was taking the action to stop

---

21 Meta fined 390 over use of data in targeted ads, Chris Vallance, https://www.bbc.com/news/technology-64153383.

people losing money to clickbait advertising scams, such as ones using his image to promote cryptocurrency schemes. The lawsuit filed by Forrest alleges Facebook 'failed to create controls or a corporate culture to prevent its systems being used to commit crime', and that Facebook was 'criminally reckless' by not taking sufficient steps to stop criminals from using its social media platform to send scam advertisements to defraud Australian users.[22] [23]

Numerous companies have been fined under Europe's General Data Protection Regulations including Meta, Google, Amazon, Facebook, H&M, Enel Energia, British Airways and Marriott. Over the 2021–22 financial year the number of GDPR violations increased 113.5% while the number of fines increased 124.92%.[24]

Misuse aside, business leaders need to have a laser-sharp focus on the use case. If you are giving customers choice about what data you capture in a transparent way, explain why and what it will be used for today and tomorrow. Have a value exchange for them that is tangible, so that a great deal of the data angst might be removed. I don't mind Waze knowing where I'm going, as the value of their traffic information is helpful and offsets my concerns about them knowing my destination. It's a trade-off, my data for navigational information in return. It's when the value is not a fair trade that the angst arises. Beware, reputational impacts await poor use cases.

In a recent Pivot podcast, Kara Swisher and Professor Scott Galloway talked about Apple's latest move into health, specifically mental health, using data from Apple Watches. Swisher noted that it was possible to predict with a higher level of accuracy signs of depression from a lack of action through Apple devices. She was of the view that this was a step too far in terms of data privacy. Galloway had the opposite view: 'If Apple can help a customer they should.' He noted that his watch already told him when it was time to stand up. Why wouldn't it not notice that you haven't moved much today, and that you could be feeling bad as a consequence? That's actually a good thing. He made the point that what you need is regulation about how the data is used because if it's used by the consumer who has opted in to get help that's good. If Apple misuses the data, they're liable for court cases to get sued for loss, and you need judges to enforce the privacy laws.

22 https://www.afr.com/technology/andrew-forrest-sues-facebook-over-scam-ads-20220203-p59tlw.

23 https://www.watoday.com.au/national/western-australia/andrew-forrest-clears-major-legal-hurdle-in-facebook-clickbait-court-case-20221018-p5bqsm.html.

24 Ibid.

Let's take another example. In Australia, where I live, well before the advent of the internet the government made it illegal to price health insurance on a risk basis for the individual. This means that if a smoking, beer-guzzling, non-exerciser compares their health insurance costs to a teetotalling fitness nut there will be almost no difference in price. Australia's private health insurance system is community rated not risk rated by the individual. This ensures all people get the same price for a policy no matter their age, gender or health status. This policy takes all the data arbitrage out.

It's also a good example of where regulation got ahead of the advances in data analysis capabilities. Today, you could predict with reasonable accuracy the body mass index (BMI) of households based on their location relative to fresh food and fast-food restaurants, heat maps of credit card expenditure on gym memberships, and thousands of other data points that are available. In Australia's case, sound, timely regulation meant the incentives to price the health risk was removed. Add in a DNA sample and you could predict a great deal of health issues for the individual.

This policy has a positive effect on the health insurers because their best lever to increase profits is in helping their customers stay well and keep fit. Innovation in this area has flourished with wellness apps, and linkages of these apps to health insurance companies. Discovery Limited, a South African-based financial services group, is the global master of this, and I share this example story in Chapter 7. Suffice to say here, one of their promotions is subsidised Apple Watches, which are then linked (with the customer's permission) to health and wellness apps and vital information. The value of this data exchange is shared between the company and the customer.

It is an example of where the use case for the customer – being healthier – also aligns with the company as healthier customers mean fewer claims on their insurance. There is real value created and real value attributed to the customer and shared with the customer. This value exchange is front and centre of their marketing.

On 8 February 2023, Microsoft CEO Satya Nadella revealed some of Microsoft's new initiatives around AI integration into their products. He cited this use case:

> A farmer, speaking in Hindi, expresses a pretty complex thought about how he had heard about some government program and wants to apply for a subsidy that he thinks he's eligible for. It's a pretty complex prompt query. But this technology does a good job. It goes to the bot that recognises the speech comes back and says 'You know what, you should go to this portal, fill out these forms and you will get your subsidy.' So he says, 'Look, I'm not going to go into any portal. I'm not going to fill out any forms. Can you help me?' And it does it.

The Microsoft CEO went on to explain how they built a daisy chain model of trained AI that worked out how to find the relevant government websites and then how to apply for grants for the farmers. It also used speech recognition to allow those with low literacy to solve their needs.

Boards need to be asking, now that these tools are available, what can their organisations create with this new sort of capability? As the democratising of AI tools unfolds what will your organisation do? How will it help your customers and meet their changing needs?

For example, traditional travel companies allow you to book airfares and accommodation, insurance and more. The customer bears the risk of weather. Yet, an AI-enabled travel booking engine could be built to allow the user to book a holiday at a budget and time that is, for example, optimised for good weather. It adjusts the bookings to the weather of your trip. You book your week of leave and set a budget, set some criteria, such as good beaches and restaurants. It scans for deals and weather-optimised bookings and rebook-ings inside of cancellation deadlines for your benefit, with some last-minute booking options thrown in. The days of you researching holidays could be over. Your bot, with your best interests guiding it, could do this. Feed it your favourite photos from your last trip and it could find places 'like that' for your next trip. When you stop and think about new business models using AI they are endless, and we will see many come in the near term as AI: Game On becomes fully enabled.

Are we on the verge of all having personal agents finding truth without bias and bringing it home to us? Or are we heading for more AI-enabled mis-information? We don't know, but we will find out. Regulators need to help the former and stop the latter.

The over-collection of data is growing and is rapidly becoming out of control. There have been stories in the press recently about how a bread retailer is not allowing customers to buy bread without giving the retailer their email. Why? To force people into some low-value loyalty system, which is all about the business being able to target the customer but has little or no value to the customer.

A couple of personal examples. I went to lease an investment property and the forms stated that I had to give them permission to use my private information in the media. Sure, it was on the fourth page of the terms and conditions in font size 6. Why? There is no reason, other than if you happened to be Tom Cruise, they would want to leverage your profile. Yet, here it was as a standard condition.

Recently, I was looking to make an investment in a new fund, where I know the managers and believe in their capability. So, I filled out the forms, and was then asked to provide my passport as part of the Know Your Customer (KYC) protocols set up to 'know me' and also inhibit money laundering. Its aim is fair enough, but the idea of sending a photo of my passport to an email address I have not used before was too much for me, so I said no. In fact, I asked them to give me directors' guarantees that in the event they are hacked, and I suffer loss, they will cover my losses. Guess what? They would do no such thing.

A large-scale electrical retailer sent me an email about the urgent recall of a product I bought from them saying there was a fire risk and serious damage or death could result. I asked them to take the product back, and they then asked me for their model number and photos of the compliance plate. It was not a scam, but does show their data strategy is a mess, as they clearly don't know which customer has which model of their product. It's lazy, sloppy and will result in litigation. Where is the board? Data is too important to be left with the data department.

Society is going to need a way through this, as Rachel Botsman explores in *Who Can You Trust?* The 2022 Optus and Medicare data breaches in Australia show how private information of customers (even past customers of up to five years) is now vulnerable to criminals who are out to auction the data to other criminals. Cyber theft is a global business, and billions of dollars are being spent to mitigate the threat, as it should be. A more important question for all businesses must be: What information do we actually need to benefit the customer? Does my real estate agent need to be able to tell the media about my house? Does the coffee shop need to send me special offers I don't want or a retail outlet an electronic receipt so they can add me to their marketing database? Thoughtfulness and empathy from leaders has never been needed more than it is today.

We got to this position as businesses focused on what they wanted to use data for, not for what's in the best interest of the customer. And the result? A massive line-up of class actions that will, in an odd way, hopefully force boards and executives to pay more attention to their data and AI. In short, if the organisation collects data, it better have a good reason to do so, a good use case for the customer, and exceptionally good data protections.

It's the use case, stupid

Executives and managers need to get better at asking: Where is the customer in the use case? Why is this good for them? How do we protect them from poor first-, second- or third-order consequences from our data use? How do we contain the data and keep it out of the wild? If your propriety data gets out in the OpenAI world your advantage is now everyone's.

To highlight some of the issues here, consider OpenAI and the large language models (LLMs) being used. Some useful metrics on OpenAI come from the *Australian Financial Review* on 24 January 2023 quoted below:

> With each new generation of LLMs, the number of parameters has been ballooning, starting with 117 million in GPT and 340 million in BERT. GPT-3, the LLM on which OpenAI based ChatGPT, has 175 billion parameters. Google's GLaM (Generalist Language Model) has 1.2 trillion.
>
> The result is a kind of magic: machines that have ingested an internet's worth of data, weighed up the relationships between things, and are able to generate content that appears to be new and original.

The article went on to explain how LLMs with billions, and moving to trillions, of parameters can still create effects that AI researcher Emily Bender described as "stochastic parrots". They seem intelligent, yet don't understand the words they are creating. A human looks for meaning, while currently, models look for patterns.[25]

Machines may already know you better than you know yourself, at least your consumption habits

If you ask most people what they spent on subscription services last month, many will dramatically underestimate the recurring costs they pay to streaming companies and others. Or ask your friend what their favourite cuisine is and then get them to look at their bank statements of what cuisine they paid for the most in the last three months. Often our own recollection of real behaviours can be wrong. It's a bias in our mind as opposed to the reality of our bank statements. It also shows that banks can know us better than we know ourselves in many instances. What could a bank do for its customers with the data they have?

Imagine if you could travel to a new town, walk into a restaurant and see what someone like you who eats regularly in that restaurant orders frequently.

---

25   https://www.afr.com/technology/is-chatgpt-a-form-of-magic-or-the-apocalypse-20230117-p5cd4p.

It could reveal the best meal in the house, not what some random person has stated on a website that is full of spam and self-interest. Loyalty is usually a measure of customer satisfaction and banks can see loyalty clearly at scale if they have systems set up to help and understand their customers.

Years ago at Quantium, they built an app called People Like You for UBank. It used de-identified bank data and you could find some highly predictive information in this data set. I looked at the pizza restaurants in my postcode for people of similar age and income to me. To my amazement they all were going to this very small pizza place that was hidden off the main street that I liked too. I thought I was special! Google searches did not reveal this restaurant as this low-key place had no SEO or AdWords dollars. The bank data found what Google could not see – we are what we do.

Banks have been using the same credit models for generations, and even with the new laws around Know Your Customer (KYC), banks still ask borrowers to labour through reams of questions that they already know the answer to. How much do you spend on food? You say $200 a week for the family. They know it is $230 but don't use their own – your own – data. It is changing in some banks, but it's generally seen as too hard, and their systems are old; they suffer from inertia and push the hard work to the customer and use claimed behaviour over real behaviour. Netflix knows I don't watch documentaries about post-modern art. Ask people in a survey or focus groups and you will hear lots of noise of good intentions or virtue signalling over real customer signals.

Here's a test that I often use in discussions around data guard rails with organisations.

1. Are they legal?
2. Are they ethical?
3. Does anyone lose as a consequence of the use case?
4. Is it helpful to those whose data you are using?
5. Does the customer agree the data helps them?
6. If all your use cases were in the public domain, is this a 'story'?

Would any part of this plan be troubling for you, your stakeholders or society if an investigative journalist found the data use case? If what is being planned needs to be hidden from public scrutiny or even internal scrutiny, don't do it. The use case needs to be your North Star.

Let me run some scenarios past you, and ask yourself how comfortable you feel. Please note, these are clearly personal choices and there will be different views:

- You are asked if your de-identified health data could be used to find a new way of preventing/treating cancer. (Sounds okay, so long as I can pull my data if I want to or not, and there is zero risk of PI (personal data being identified or obtained). If there was a breakthrough and large financial win from the data, is there a share split with the data provided?)

- Having your car's braking data used to help design better brakes. (Good, so long as it can't be used against me in an insurance claim, or a police matter.)

- Your movie streaming preferences are being used to find more of what you want to watch. (Good, thanks, so long as no one else can see my own viewing preferences.)

- Your shopping data being used to help the retailers stock the right items for you and others. (Good, so long as it's not on-sold for insurance, or other second-order users that could erode my benefits or irritate me.)

- Health data being used by an insurance company to inform them of your health risks, so they can increase premiums. (Not good. A simple no.)

- An online retailer using your data in a way that shows your preferences are for premium wines, and they offer discounts to other customers who show greater price sensitivity discounts on some of the same premium wines, effectively leaving you in the sucker segment paying full price. (Bad use of customer data as it puts their interests ahead of the customers.)

- The government or platforms using/selling your social media data to predict who you will vote for and target you with messages to persuade you to switch your vote. (We hate this, yet it is used and both sides of politics use social media to try and predict voting intentions. It's the use case, transparency of the user's data and who gets the benefits of the data use that matter in the end.)

There is a growing, legitimate interest from individuals regarding the data they provide to various organisations. In short, there does need to be a real value exchange to keep the balance right.

Transparent notices on what the data is being used for are needed. Surprising customers with a bad use of their data is not a sustainable strategy. For example, sharing my family's data on our use of streaming services gives the streaming company real insights into what shows to make next, what to change, and where to advertise for like programs and more. The users (my family) get great recommendations at a minimum, and you could argue they will also get a pipeline of new content they are likely to enjoy. So, there is some mutual value.

However, when our data is used to create large-scale value in second-order use cases the matter becomes more complex. If the use of our search data shows market trends that enable real estate developments to outperform, where is the share in the upside? Should this be part of the value exchange if an entrepreneur has the courage to put investment at risk on that data?

By contrast, if the data is widely available then is this just market data, like Census or other data sets, and not using the data becomes a business risk. If the data is not available widely, such as viewing habit data of streaming, and if the use case is not transparent to those whose data is shared that is another matter.

Not all insights from search or other data lead to gold-plated business outcomes. There are examples of data-driven economic loss. The risk and reward balance needs consideration. If companies use precious customer data and do not give back value they will soon find new competitors that use customer data for better use cases for the customer. They will also see new business models where data privacy is part of the differentiation of products and services. Apple sees iPhone data privacy as a strong way to differentiate from other phones. Transparency and a data Hippocratic oath are key to staying on the right side of the data value exchange.

As data can be stored forever, a question that should be asked is: If we store this data for this one purpose, then reuse it for another, who will authorise that use, and ensure the above scenarios are answered, and that the data Hippocratic oath can be kept?

Data collection, use, sharing and policy

Walid Khiari, an investment banker in Palo Alto, explained to me at breakfast one morning, 'The old world was policy driving adoption. The new world is adoption driving policy.'

Uber anyone? Over 2 million Australians had downloaded the Uber app and were actively using the service before governments had meaningful discussion about its impact on taxi license plates, which they had sold to taxi owners. Adoption is now the driver of policy in too many places, illustrating how regulators are too often late to the party or rather society's needs. The party may be being held by large tech companies that are extracting massive value out of new ways of engaging people. The consequences of misinformation, too much screen time and second-order impacts are pushed on to society.

Adoption driving policy is not a healthy position for society to be in, and we need regulators to step up and get into the fast lane of tech developments. The best time to legislate for how the next generation of AI/data/tech companies use data is before it starts, not when billions of people are using it daily.

When social media began, were any regulators ready for this new world? Which government departments were thinking about the trillions of data points that would flow, and the predictive and addictive attributes that would be available to the owners?

Now with tools like OpenAI and its ChatGPT outputs and more, there are increasing levels of concern around copyright and other areas where the laws lag well behind the adoption cycle. If you are a writer or content creator what are the chances your work is in OpenAI? Odds are your content is now in the vast content soup that can be trawled and used. Amazon has many new book titles for sale written by AI; much of this has been derived from the AI looking at existing authors' work. *I Forced a Bot to Write This Book* is one such title.

The current debate about whether we should pause AI development is a rational debate to be had. What it seems to miss is the use case imperative. If the use case is to help humanity, would we want to pause it? Or if the use case to create division, hatred and misinformation or other bad use cases perhaps we should pause. If AI can help identify moles that are pre-cancerous, for example, that is very different to use cases that lead to teen depression.

Regulators are a long way back in the thinking here and we need more regulators at the AI planning table.

The right to be forgotten is now law in several countries. It was only needed once computers could remember everything. Now we have AI that can detect human emotions, and the use of this emotional observation is open to misuse. There is currently no policy response to many of these AI advances. Developing the use case is key.

Mira Murati, CTO at OpenAI, the company that developed ChatGPT, recently expressed her concerns about the chatbot and said that AI can be misused. '[AI] can be misused, or it can be used by bad actors. So, then there are questions about how you govern the use of this technology globally. How do you govern the use of AI in a way that's aligned with human values?' she asked in an interview with *Time* magazine. Murati added that AI should be regulated by the governments.

In a Sam Harris podcast, titled 'The Trouble with AI,' he talks to Gary Marcus, bestselling author of *Rebooting AI* and founder of Geometric Intelligence, and Stuart Russell, Professor of Computer Science at Berkeley and Director of the Center for Human-Compatible AI. It's a two-hour podcast and a fascinating conversation about AI challenges and where we're at in terms of artificial general intelligence (AGI).

Some key takeaways from this are:

1. Testing what happens with AI on millions or billions of people is not ethical. We would not allow this in food or pharmaceuticals. There are regulations that are enforceable and risk mitigation measures in place. Yet we allow tech companies to do R&D in the wild with little more than reputational consequences at present.

2. Cessation of research is very hard to enforce and apply. But it has happened – genetic engineers were gung-ho about improving the human gene pool 50 years ago, yet by the mid-1970s they had pulled back. As of now there are no human clones. I make the point again, it's about the use case, as using DNA to modify cancer cells is happening and is not seen as a threat like creating a clone army.

3. Views on the timeline to any real AGI are different. It's clearly impossible to know when and if this materialises. Various experts do think it will be here in some form and make the point that so far the rollout of AI has not gone smoothly and lack of thoughtful regulations is not a good sign for what may await in AGI and other AI use.[26]

I wonder how many regulators attend South by Southwest (SXSW) to watch the birth of new industries, or subscribe to Crunchbase to follow where the early capital is being allocated and what is waiting downstream from these deals for society. It is time to demand more from the entrepreneurs running these businesses to ensure their businesses align with humanity's interest, and to call for more from the regulators who will need to stay in front to protect society from bad actors and unintended consequences.

There are rapidly shifting expectations about how data can be collected, used and shared, both from the individuals whose data it is and the companies that are amassing and using it to deliver services to the customer. As customers become more knowledgeable about the value of their data, the onus is on organisations to ensure it is fit for purpose and that purpose can't be solely profit above the customers' interests or those of society.

Large ecosystems of shared data have formed into massive data lakes and increasingly gigantic oceans.

Some are of the highest standards, where real thought has gone into making the data de-identified, privacy compliant, and encrypted to the highest standards attaining ISO ratings and other metrics to show compliance with GDPR standards and more.

---

26 Read more at: https://economictimes.indiatimes.com/tech/technology/chatgpt-who-is-mira-murati-and-why-she-believes-ai-should-be-regulated/articleshow/97804074.cms?utm_source=contentofinterest&utm_medium=text&utm_campaign=cppst.

Others operate on the dark web and are a jungle of personal information gained through cybercrime and other nefarious means. There are some significant initiatives and not-for-profit organisations building platforms for data sharing.

Gaia-X is one such data-sharing project backed by the European Union and the Gaia-X Association for Data and Cloud.[27] An interoperable data exchange, Gaia-X allows businesses to share data under the protection of strict European data privacy laws.[28] Europe has the GDPR (General Data Protection Regulation) while, odd as it may seem, the USA doesn't have the equivalent of Europe's GDPR, rather a patchwork of historical privacy provisions in various areas, including the US Privacy Act of 1974, 1996, the Health Insurance Portability and Accountability Act (HIPAA), the 2000 Children's Online Privacy Protection Act (COPPA), the Gramm-Leach-Bliley Act, the Californian Consumer Privacy Act (CCPA), along with a raft of other state acts.[29]

In Australia, the federal government is investing in expansion of the consumer data right rules (CDR), infrastructure and skills to drive standards for emerging technologies such as artificial intelligence, quantum computing and 6G mobility. It rightly sees consumer data rights as critical to promoting greater mobility and richer service options for users when choosing their bank, energy or telecommunication providers.[30] In Australia we're starting to see the early results of open banking, which allows customers to instruct their bank (and soon energy retailers and telcos) to send their data to a competitor or niche provider, who could use it to price or create better services.

The push to expand the CDR is part of a broader plan to lift data capability with the aim of promoting greater data sharing and asset management. For example, Geoscience Australia has been provided with $40 million to develop a three-dimensional digital atlas of Australia's geography, bringing together public data on people, the economy, employment, infrastructure, health, land and the environment into a single national data asset. There's also a $16.5 million pilot program to make government data assets more discoverable. This program will develop data inventories for 20% of Commonwealth agencies, and shared digital infrastructure and standards for a publicly available catalogue of government data assets.

Intergovernmental data is a real challenge. The state governments in Australia are responsible for state police and all road fatality data is held at a state level.

---

27 https://www.gaia-x.eu/who-we-are/association.

28 https://www.technologyreview.com/2021/10/19/1037290/getting-value-from-your-data-shouldnt-be-this-hard/.

29 https://www.varonis.com/blog/us-privacy-laws.

30 https://www.senatorhume.com/latest-news-folder/media-releases/consumer-data-right-rolled-out-to-the-energy-sector.

The Australian Government is interested in understanding and helping to reduce road accidents and would ideally like to link the state data sets to form a national view. The nuances in these data sets hold the keys to safer roads. To help reduce the terrible burden of road accidents we need to have real attribution data as to the real cause of each accident.

There can be multiple factors in a road death. Factors include the condition of the road, the weather at the time (was the sun in a driver's eyes?) the type of car, the driver's age, and speed, fatigue of the driver and so on. These data sets are rich, and, if linked and reviewed with powerful analytics, their yield will be lives saved and infrastructure spending aligned to better safety. Sharing data to save lives should be easy, but silos and bureaucracy make this hard for now.

When you look at data that is captured in a road accident it is rudimentary, and I suspect we miss lead and lag indicators. As cars increase in sophistication, they will have more data on board, increasingly like a black box flight recorder. Where is this data being used for road safety? Some early initiatives exist in the USA, but it's a long way from scaled real insights. If a driver has had their traffic-side mirror hit twice, is that a near head-on, a near-fatality miss? It could be, but the data is not there to analyse. If a truck on a mine site had a mirror clipped that data would, in many cases, be used as a way to understand near-miss fatalities. We need to think a lot more as a society about how to use this sort of information to help make a safer world. It can be done in a privacy compliant way that protects the individual.

Unintended or unethical data use

There are countless examples of data and machine learning algorithms having been misused and abused – either intentionally or unintentionally. In 2022, the Australian Government held a parliamentary subcommittee into social media and online safety. Frances Haugen, a Facebook whistle-blower, was invited to give evidence. Haugen had previously leaked documents and gave damning testimony to a US congressional committee. Haugen said the company knew the algorithms underpinning products on Facebook and Instagram were sowing misinformation and harming children, but that executives had 'put astronomical profits' ahead of safety. She has urged the Australian parliamentary subcommittee to 'regulate the heart of the business model of the platforms – the algorithms and design features that allow dis-information and hate to be spread and for the exploitation of personal data.'[31] Here are a few more examples.

---

31   https://www.afr.com/politics/federal/operating-in-the-dark-facebook-whistleblower-warns-of-election-risk-20220203-p59tip.

1. **Amazon's AI recruiting tool** – The tool developed for hiring by Amazon started to bias against female job applicants.[32]

2. The **Australian Government's** Online Compliance Intervention, commonly known as Robodebt, was later judged to be an unlawful method of automated debt assessment and recovery employed by Services Australia as part of its Centrelink payment compliance program. The scheme aimed to replace the manual system of calculating overpayments and issuing debt notices to welfare recipients. The new idea was to use an automated data-matching system that compared Centrelink records with averaged income data from the Australian Taxation Office, which was a method found to be unlawful. It started in 2016, and it was terminated in 2020, with the Australian Government paying $1.2 billion in compensation as a result of a class action.[33]

3. **Microsoft's** Twitter bot named Tay, based on an ML algorithm that was meant to get smarter the more users interacted with it, got corrupted within 24 hours from its launch with the supply of misogynistic, racist messages from Twitter.[34]

4. **Google's** hate speech detector – Google's AI tool developed to catch hate speeches started to behave differently towards Black people.[35]

In terms of outright misuse and abuse of data, consider the following examples:

1. **Cambridge Analytica**. In early 2014, Cambridge Analytica, a British political consulting firm, signed a deal with Aleksandr Kogan for a private venture that would capitalise on the work of Michal Kosinski and his team. Kogan created a quiz, thanks to an initiative at Facebook that allowed third parties to access user data. Almost 300,000 users were estimated to have taken that quiz. It later emerged that Cambridge Analytica then exploited the data it had harvested via the quiz to access and build profiles for 87 million Facebook users. Some claim neither Facebook nor Cambridge Analytica's decisions were strictly illegal. According to Julian Wheatland, COO of Cambridge Analytica at the time, the company's biggest mistake was believing that complying with government regulations was enough, and thereby ignoring broader questions of data ethics, bias and public perception.[36]

---

32 https://www.reuters.com/article/us-amazon-com-jobs-automation-insight/amazon-scraps-secret-ai-recruiting-tool-that-showed-bias-against-women-idUSKCN1MK08G.

33 https://en.wikipedia.org/wiki/Robodebt_scheme.

34 https://www.theverge.com/2016/3/24/11297050/tay-microsoft-chatbot-racist.

35 https://futurism.com/the-byte/google-hate-speech-ai-biased.

36 https://hbr.org/2019/11/does-your-ai-have-users-best-interests-at-heart.

2. In September 2019, **Twitter** admitted to letting advertisers access its users' personal data to improve the targeting of marketing campaigns. Cited by the company as an internal error,[37] the bug allowed Twitter's Tailored Audiences advertisers access to user email addresses and phone numbers. Twitter's ad buyers could then cross-reference their marketing database with Twitter's to identify shared customers and serve them targeted ads – all without their permission.

3. In 2020 hackers accessed 5.2 million **Marriott** guest records including customer contact information, personal preferences, birthdays and more. This attack succeeded because the attackers compromised employee credentials to access a third-party application. While more a case of data theft than abuse, it was two months before anyone realised it had occurred, resulting in a significant breach of trust for Marriott.

Interestingly, three of the leading tech players, namely IBM, Google and Microsoft, have turned down projects due to ethical concerns. Google cloud experts agreed not to move forward with the idea of creating AI for financial institutions to make decisions for lending money. The project was put on hold until the concerns regarding gender and racial biases were resolved. Microsoft, too, limits the use of its software that mimics voice amid concerns about using the technique for creating deep fakes. Similarly, sensing the possibility of misuse, IBM discontinued its face recognition services altogether.

There is a robust global discussion around the ethics that must underpin the collection of data and the development of AI and machine learning. Most governments are now racing to develop and implement regulations, reporting and accountability for data use and AI. That said, no amount of regulation and laws replace the concept of individual and collective corporate responsibility for the ethical use of data.

The founder of the internet, Tim Berners-Lee, said, 'Data is a precious thing and will last longer than the systems it runs on.' Boards are on notice that poor data use, hygiene and misuse is a place of class actions and regulatory scrutiny.

The head of the UK House of Lords Select Committee on AI, Lord Clement-Jones, shared the core of that committee's recommendations – five ethical principles which, it says, should be applied across sectors, nationally and internationally:

- Artificial intelligence should be developed for the common good and benefit of humanity.

- Artificial intelligence should operate on principles of intelligibility and fairness.

---

37 https://help.twitter.com/en/information-and-ads.

- Artificial intelligence should not be used to diminish the data rights or privacy of individuals, families or communities.
- All citizens should have the right to be educated to enable them to flourish mentally, emotionally and economically alongside artificial intelligence.
- The autonomous power to hurt, destroy or deceive human beings should never be vested in artificial intelligence.[38]

Uncontrolled entrepreneurial activity could take us to some dark places. The use case needs to be aligned with the ethical principles above. There are some use cases from which humanity may struggle to recover. The human genome is so powerful when used for good health advancement, yet so concerning if used to modify humans for a purpose that is not aligned with humanity's best interest.

Once the atomic bomb was developed, tested and used, its impact was known and it has had consequences for generations. Whatever you think of the ethical nature of this weapon, just who has the right to develop such technology today needs to be carefully thought through by everyone. And rules, guidelines and regulations (preferably global) need to be formed, enacted and monitored. In a world where AI is dispersed and discovered globally within an instant, much thought needs to be given to the ethical principles and a regulatory framework applied across the whole of the data and AI spectrum.

Bias in AI and human decision-making

Much of the discussion in the business and wider community around AI is focused on the conscious and unconscious bias that *may* be in the algorithms that are being deployed by organisations, and how these *might* positively or negatively impact the outcomes of various interactions.

Machines can make bad decisions and they can be at scale. But humans make a lot of bad decisions based on emotion, unconscious biases, incomplete information, and the inability to absorb large quantities and different sources of information.

When we compare algorithmic decisions to decisions that humans make, we often get the baselines wrong. For example, let's consider how Tesla has faced real pressure, as it should, for the fatalities that have occurred with their self-driving mode. The day that the first Tesla crashed in the USA and killed someone it was worldwide news. That day there were more than 90 other road fatalities, and an average of over 100 deaths occur each day on roads in the

USA, a human baseline that is tragic yet rarely questioned. Of all these human driving catastrophes there is little data to understand just why these happened. Whereas in the Tesla crash, there are tens of thousands of data points to help Tesla continuously improve how the car operates. It's useful that Tesla publishes information about all crashes on its website.[39]

In 2021, a staggering 42,000-plus fatalities were recorded on American roads. The forensic understanding of these tragedies is hard to unpack as combinations of events are common: low light, poor road conditions, speed, alcohol, fatigue, cars with bald tyres, and on goes the list of factors that add up to each of these tragic events.

There is very little scrutiny into the nature of the human decisions behind the errors that lead to 42,000 'non-Tesla' deaths. In contrast, Tesla systems learn from driving behaviours, car behaviours and local situations all the time, in real time. Humans know only our own driving techniques. Worse still, we tend to teach our own children to drive. If the parent has a bad habit, it can easily be transferred to the next generation. If the driverless car has an incident, it can be coded to avoid that mistake and avoid it forever more.

Tesla's ability to optimise its autopilot grows exponentially faster than a human undertaking driver training.

In Australia, there's the same paucity of actual data about car crashes. A great deal of the cause or effect data would be available in all self-driving cars but not via human assessments (police and car crash investigators). 'Better data will outperform better algorithms,' says Adam Driussi, CEO, co-founder and CEO of Quantium. 'Combined, the best data and best algorithms are very hard to beat.' The best result is to ensure both the algorithms and the data being used are of the highest standard.

We humans have biases, both conscious and unconscious, and we make decisions and mistakes that are hard to audit – we are impossible to reprogram at scale.

Good data and AI governance must allow the data analytics and any actual or perceived biases and mistakes to be evaluated, audited, repaired and reprogrammed. AI has the capacity to be more robust and less biased than humans, and getting bias out of AI decision-making is a key priority. The reality is that AI has inherited biases from people, as people create them. Computer scientist Melvin Conway PhD developed what is known as Conway's law, which states that 'organisations which design systems are constrained to produce designs which are copies of the communication structures of these organisations.'[40]

---

39 https://www.tesla.com/VehicleSafetyReport.

40 https://www.fastcompany.com/90356295/the-rush-toward-ethical-ai-is-leaving-many-of-us-behind.

That is, if a team developing a particular AI system is made up of similar types of people who rely on similar first principles, the resulting output is likely to reflect that.

Conway's law exists within educational institutions as well. In training technology students on ethics, institutions are mostly taking what's been dubbed a 'Silicon Valley approach' to AI ethics that is structured around a single cultural frame that reinforces a white, male Western perspective taught to and therefore influencing younger, male minds who make up the bulk of data scientists, AI and machine learning specialists. What this might mean is that the ethics underpinning digital technology and associated regulatory and ethical frameworks of worldwide are essentially biased.

In a 2021 article, Emmanuel R. Goffi discussed the importance of cultural diversity in AI ethics, noting that the West accounts for 63% of the codes relating to the ethics of AI. According to the authors of 'The Global Landscape of AI Ethics Guidelines', this over-representation indicates a lack of global equality in the treatment of AI and shows that the most economically advanced countries are shaping the debate by 'neglecting local knowledge, cultural pluralism and global fairness.' Goffi suggests that 'We need to open the discussion about the ethical rules of AI up to different cultures and, therefore, different philosophical perspectives.' It makes for uncomfortable reading to recognise that much of the discussion around AI, data and ethics is Western-dominated, largely leaving out the different cultural and philosophical perspectives and constructs of the likes of Asia, China, India, Latin America, Africa and the Middle East.[41]

Regulation and oversight

In November 2023, Bletchley Park in England, the iconic WW2 code-breaking centre, hosted the world's top technology powers. At this meeting there was a pledge to jointly tackle the potentially catastrophic harms of artificial intelligence. Over 25 countries attended to attempt to set aside geopolitical rivalries and competing ideas on how to govern the rise of the machines. The US, the European Union, China, India and 25 other mostly Asian and Gulf countries attended to align on key issues relating to AI safety.

While the focus of this chapter is always acting in the best interests of the customer in relation to data and AI, there is an increasingly global regulatory framework being developed to protect individual privacy and ownership of personal data. There's still a long way to go here. We need to be hopeful that regulators and governments can keep up with the rapid advancement of AI

---

41   https://behorizon.org/the-importance-of-cultural-diversity-in-ai-ethics/.

and machine learning. They have made real progress in relation to the ownership of personal data, with differences depending on the country you live in.

As a company that is capturing and utilising data through AI and machine learning, you'll be developing intellectual property that can have significant value. Your other high-value assets, like the tangible assets, have someone in the organisation who knows a lot about them, where they are, how they work, what risks sit in them. Now that data and AI have such value, make sure the organisation can answer the same sort of questions about this class of assets. Here are some questions to start with:

- How does it work and create value?
- Is it ethically sound?
- Did the customer authorise the use of their data and for what purposes?
- What risks are incurred by storing this data?
- What second- or third-order consequences could come about from using the data?

AI that is working well should be identified as IP and sit on your asset and risk register, as this will mean the board is aware of its value and how to protect it.

If you are losing, because of a lack of innovation about AI, that fact should be on your risk register.

I end this chapter with the data Hippocratic oath.

We will do no harm with the data we collect.
We will not use the information about any human being for any
purpose that makes life harder for those we are here to serve.
We will respect the privacy of our customers, and not allow
information about them to be used against them in any way.

With the foundation of the data Hippocratic oath in mind, it's now time to explore the potential futures out there for your organisation and industry. The following chapters will help you understand what you need to do to become match fit, and become an organisation that harnesses data and AI to grow your business for the future or make your organisation more effective and efficient.

CHAPTER TAKEAWAYS

1. Cybersecurity is crucial for businesses, and trust with customers is fragile, so companies should focus on building and maintaining trust.

2. Just as insurers can increase profits by helping customers stay healthy, AI technology can be used to create new business models in all industries that align with the best interests of customers.

3. There are rapidly changing expectations around data collection, use and sharing, and regulators need to get ahead of tech developments and legislate to protect society from bad actors.

4. Ethical concerns must be taken seriously by company directors.

5. AI technology can often make better decisions than humans, but bias exists in both AI and human decision-making, so we need to be empathetic and careful about how we develop and deploy new technology.

Chapter 4

KNOW YOUR CUSTOMER

'There is absolutely no inevitability, so long as there is a willingness to contemplate what is happening.' – Marshall McLuhan, Canadian philosopher

"I believe fundamentally that organisations like ours and others will be successful if they solve the future problems that customers have. If they don't, they'll just go out of business.' – Michael Dell

Watching streaming TV or the TV watching me

As of September 2023, Netflix has 247 million paid subscribers.[42] When someone signs up it asks for your interests and preferences. Its algorithms also track what you watch, the completion rate, the common cut-off point; when you pause, rewind or fast forward; what day you watch content (Netflix has found people watch TV shows during the week and movies during the weekend); the date you watched, what time you watched; where you watch (zip/postcode); what device you use to watch (do you like to use your tablet for TV shows and your Roku for movies?. Do people access the Just for Kids feature more on their iPads etc.?); when you pause and leave content (and if you ever come back); the ratings given (about 4 million per day); searches (about 3 million per day); browsing and scrolling behaviour, even the data within movies. Traditional television networks don't have access to any of this data and this is reflected in their valuations. All to say, the lack of data leads to lack of customer understanding and that leads to a lack of future cash flows and hence the negative valuation impact on free-to-air television. TV networks are now fighting back to try and recover from the data weakness with their own apps, streaming offerings and more. They were in box seat creating and in many cases owning the content; this advantage was lost when new entrants arrived that had real use data to understand the customer.

---

42 https://www.statista.com/statistics/483112/netflix-subscribers/.

Harnessing the intention and attention economy

To win in the intention and attention economy you need data and AI-enabled systems that are in tune with customer needs and have the ability to spot emerging needs. Netflix doesn't have a data business, it has a customer business. They can discern intention from their customer data and also engage you to obtain attention. Netflix has been built on the mantra of customer science, a form of science dedicated to knowing you in order to serve you. Reed Hastings, the co-founder and executive chairman of Netflix, has said that he hopes customer science will be his legacy. An AI: Game On organisation is one that is built around an ecosystem that knows each customer well enough to predict what they want and when and how they want it, to genuinely know them to serve them.

As I write, I have a text from an office supplier asking me to rank their delivery of printer cartridges. Good on them for seeking feedback. But the product never arrived, and their systems are too broken to know it. On their website, there is a range of FAQs and nothing about what to do when the delivery does not arrive. Yet I can see presentations from the CEO on customer-centricity as their number one goal. Without a data spine that enables visibility into the customer's real situation at a granular level, it's just a guessing game, and rhetoric about being a customer-centric company is promising a standard with no chance of living up to it.

They have the customer's cash, and so now this is all the customer's problem. Nice for them, but it will guarantee large-scale defection. Do their data systems see this link? It should and could, but if the culture of the company is like this one, they will be eaten alive by the companies that get this right and stay in tune with the real customer experience. As I ditch this poor service provider and aim my browser at Amazon, I feel for the employees trapped in this Australian domiciled business that has not figured out how to make their data spine work for their customers. That is on the board and CEO, and boards need to step up to ensure their organisations are globally competitive as we are all just one click away from a data-enabled company that creates fewer headaches for customers.

Charles Darwin's *On the Origin of Species by Means of Natural Selection* plays out in business too. Longevity at the top of the pack is shorter than ever before, as a lack of focus on the customer sees many organisations sleepwalking into Kodakville.

Only 10.2% of the Fortune 500 companies in 1955 have remained on the list up to 2020, which means more than 89% of the companies from 1955 have either gone bankrupt, merged with (or were acquired by) another firm, or they still exist but have fallen from the top Fortune 500 companies (ranked by total revenues) in one year or more.[43]

43   https://docs.google.com/document/d/1zsQ2Q27KYyUZLKcve-eRhrF6ZU2jWrsNHikD5CB9oO8/edit.

A 2016 report recorded that corporations in the S&P 500 Index in 1965 stayed in the index for an average of 33 years. By 1990, average tenure in the S&P 500 had narrowed to 20 years and is forecast to shrink to 14 years by 2026. At the current churn rate, about half of today's S&P 500 firms will be replaced over the next 10 years as 'we enter a period of heightened volatility for leading companies across a range of industries, with the next ten years shaping up to be the most potentially turbulent in modern history.'[44]

The annual reports of many large corporations claim their focus is on being customer-centric. It's the right aspiration yet we are all customers and, through that lens, we know through our lived experiences every day that it's very hard for companies to read their own labels about being customer-centric from 'the inside of their own bottle'.

Founders and executives of AI: Game On companies know this, and the story of Airbnb, which early on studied, lived as and spent time with customers who were renting short-term apartments, is a good example of what it takes. Study the customer's pain point, like where to find the keys, what to do when appliances don't work, where the closest food outlets are, transportation options and the like. This enabled them to build one of the most successful ventures of the last decade, one built on understanding and meeting the unmet needs of the customer. They have detractors of course as there are societal impacts from short-term rental of accommodation that need attention too. However, the affinity they have with their customers is well known.

The CEO of a $40 billion retailer told me he sees customer-centric data use as a return to the past. I looked at him puzzled, wondering how machine learning could be like the past. He went on to explain:

> When the business was founded it was one store, with one proprietor who knew most of the customers by name, and what sort of bread they liked, and what cut of meat. Today, we have 30 million visits a week, selling 100,000 products in thousands of locations, and we can again know each of the customers' personal preferences, and how they change.

Via the data in their loyalty card this retailer has created a personalisation engine that is helpful for their customers. It knows what type of tea they like, and if the customer buys a 10-pack or 100-pack of tea bags. The algorithm will forecast when the customer will next need tea bags, as it will for all the products the customer buys. A personalised digital shopper assistant is created for every customer. The results are phenomenal.

---

44 Corporate Longevity: Turbulence Ahead for Large Organizations, Innosight.

Building this customer-driven AI is a significant, long-term investment and a whole-of-organisation approach in terms of thinking, structure, culture, engagement and action. But the outcome of this multi-year investment into analytics has been valued at well over $1 billion in enterprise value creation. It is a machine learning system and as the executives learn more about what is possible, human creativity allows the system to be updated to find more ways to help customers. It's a flywheel of customer-centricity. To summarise:

- Customers get what they want in the location they want it.
- Customers are rewarded with loyalty points and offers specific to their needs, they experience fewer stock outages, and new products are developed for their future interests.
- Wastage of food and other products is reduced, enhancing their ESG metrics.
- Suppliers are informed about what the end customers want more of and less of.
- The retailer's market share increases via increased customer loyalty.

But this is just the beginning. It's worth a quick brainstorm to think about the possibilities once the underlying data is sorted and the customer permissions are in place to use the data to help the customers. For example, you could create new segments that are infused with the customer data sets. Next week I am hosting a dinner party and want to cook something for a friend who is vegetarian. The data can help tell me what to cook. In a de-identified way you can create a shopping list of people who shop as vegetarians; the data shares what is a good guide of what products are in season and can guide in planning the menu. Add in some generative AI, and it can enable a shopping bot to fill the basket in draft for the customer's review.

No one is as smart as everyone, and the collective intelligence of millions of shoppers is now able to be turned into a collective asset for the customers as they can tap into the ideation of all other shoppers. For example, you could ask the system what meat cuts budget-focused shoppers buy.

If your organisation is not looking at personalisation for the customer benefit, ask why? You can bet your competitors are working on how to take friction out of your customers' lives and enhance personalisation as these are now becoming table stakes.

What customer-centric does not look like

Now that I have that out of the way, let's talk about others that are floundering here, as it's much more common than the success story above.

Outsourcing the costs of looking after customers with bots via OpenAI ChatGPT or others is not an act of customer-centricity, it's a cost-saving initiative, unless the customer sees it as superior, which most don't. Sure, there is promise here with ChatGPT capabilities and other large language tools. If you're not sure, ask your customers if engaging with a bot is better than talking to a real person who can understand them clearly. If it's not better, then it's a cost saving at the expense of the customer. That may be okay, or even necessary for corporate survival, but don't pretend it's not a cost-saving exercise by dressing it up as a digital transformation project.

As a customer you've probably experienced numerous fails in customer service with humans and with bots. Have you noticed how when you search for, say, 'What does the orange flashing light on the fridge mean', you find the answer more efficiently outside the brand's website through an external search? If you go to the brand website you have to hunt around the tabs, several levels of sub-tabs, multiple PDFs, and FAQs that don't list your issue. Why is it that so many companies don't have a way for customers to search product features/operating instructions easily? The question to ask is, 'Where is the customer in this?'

How many times do you see Help and FAQ sections that are not answering your needs, and there is no better answer, or way of finding the better answer?

How many times are we asked questions by call centre operators even though they have the data on what you are calling about? You call them, and they ask you for your phone number, even though you are on your phone, and they can see the number. It gets worse.

Yet, in these and the millions of other poor customer use cases, often a board is being told by management that their business is customer-centric. It's only when you are really outside of your organisation and using the products or services that the pain is felt.

I know many board chairs who make it their business to call the call centre for their own personal dealings and use a phone that is not their own to see how customer experience really works, or go to their own company's website when a friend has an issue to see if they can resolve the issue by interacting with the bot. It's interesting what you can learn by being a customer of your own company. If you haven't done it I encourage you to have a go at being your own mystery shopper.

In today's AI: Game On world, there are tools that will prescore every customer in the call centre with tenure, lifetime value, most likely reason to call, and best next conversation to help the customer.

Signals and noise and how to spot the difference

'You learn a lot more from your customers than you do from the competition.' – Michael Dell

Signals from customers are gold and have always been the key to real customer-centricity. I worked in magazines many years ago and arguably the most successful editor in Australia at that time was the legendary Nene King. Nene would spend her weekends in supermarkets watching women pick up 'her' magazines at checkout (*Australian Women's Weekly, Women's Day*) and ask them questions such as: Why did you pick up the magazine? What on the cover prompted you to pick it up? What article were you reading? Why did you put the magazine back? That was analogue customer feedback, the point being she was obsessed with the customer and what motivated them to pick up the magazine in the first place and then purchase it, or not.

Tim Ferriss interviewed Michael Dell, the Founder of Dell Computers, in 2021.[45] Michael Dell pioneered the idea of selling computers directly to the customer. If you went back to computer sales five years before Dell, no one thought he could get consumers to buy computers directly. Yet he did, and at a massive scale. Tim Ferriss asked him why he was so focused on selling directly to the home/customer. Michael Dell responded:

> If you have 10,000 retail stores and you're trying to predict what people are going to go into those stores and buy, you can have really sophisticated AI and try to guess that, but ultimately it's just a guess, and you're having to stage and prepare all sorts of things and anticipate sales and it's going to be wrong. And, to some degree, demand is going to change, and unexpected stuff is going to happen. Whereas because you're in direct contact with that customer you have clear information, and the quality of your demand signal is perfect.

Michael Dell went on to explain how companies who are finding new ways to generate persistent signal back from customers are well placed to spot changing needs, and decode future needs of customers.[46] The magic Dell claims comes from understanding the ingredients that allow the organisation to spot unsolved customer problems.[47]

---

45 https://tim.blog/2021/09/28/michael-dell/.
46 https://tim.blog/2021/09/28/michael-dell/.
47 https://tim.blog/2021/09/28/michael-dell/.

Dominos is another example. They want you to buy pizza on their app because they want to make it easier and cheaper for you to order their pizza. They also want to learn more about you (what your pizza and related product preferences are, where you live, your email, purchasing preferences etc.). While they're keen to capture this information they will need to have their customers' interest at heart by adding value; otherwise, customers won't use the app to buy from them. Customer-centricity in terms of the experience of using the app must be great for the customer and continuously improve. Otherwise the company will see high customer churn as competitors or new entrants create better customer experience.

So, if you're going to develop an app for your product/service, or drive people to your website/call centre for purchases and support, you'd better make sure these interactions really do add value across the whole experience, and it's not simply self-serving/cost-cutting for you. Companies need to ask the question, who is this benefiting most here, the organisation or the customer?

An executive in San Francisco shared the following with me. 'There are four things that you can do with data'

1. Find customers.
2. Keep customers.
3. Understand what they want next from you.
4. Optimise your capex towards the future needs of the customer.

They are all mission-critical.

Let me share a personal experience. I share a holiday house out west of Sydney in a remote location and I was with a satellite company called Activ8me, a small Australian telco (and in fairness to them, they've been great). But we've just connected to Elon Musk's Starlink,[48] which at the time of the change was 30–40 times faster than the NBN in that location. Starlink has thousands of low-orbit satellites (and Elon Musk through SpaceX is going to launch another 40,000) while NBN has two satellites in geostationary orbit. By simply registering my address with Starlink I can secure 320 Mb download and 140 Mb upload for $40 more for a connection that is up to 40 times faster.

After calling Activ8me to cancel, the representative did the paperwork, but never asked me why I was cancelling. *The* key customer signal for Activ8me was missed and this business will sadly be hit hard as a consequence of better tech by Starlink. The representative could have asked me: 'Why are you leaving? What have we done that makes you want to leave? How can we keep you?'

---

48 https://www.starlink.com/.

The end result? Starlink is already eating the Australian government's NBN and Sky Muster-based offering, as the *Australian Financial Review (AFR)* headline in January 2022 indicates: *Elon Musk's Starlink global internet creeps onto NBN's turf.*[49] The signals (not my internet ones) have been there for a while, they just weren't picked up. When the NBN was commissioned way back in 2009, its purpose was valid, to bring the internet to remote places in Australia where the telcos would not naturally invest. I remember having a meal with a group of tech-focused executives and we all concluded the $40–60 billion NBN would be soon be outpaced for many users before it was completed. It was a prediction based on what the future tech supply might look like (like Elon's new satellite and 6G), the speed at which this was changing, and some knowledge of 5G. The *AFR* reported in late 2022, 'The only surprising aspect of acknowledgement that NBN Co will never deliver a commercial return for taxpayers is how many years it took to admit the obvious.'[50] Adoption outpaced policy again.

Between 69% and 80% of online shopping orders are abandoned (not converted into a purchase),[51] and the rate differs depending on the device being used. Mobile and tablet devices have the highest percentage of shoppers hitting the exit button on a checkout page: desktop 69.75%, mobile 85.65%, tablets 80.74%. Different countries experience different abandonment rates and the cost of the item as well as the type of item also impacts the rate.[52]

Think about this. Of 100 people who head to your website to buy your product or service only 20–30 complete the transaction. If you could understand why potential customers weren't completing their transactions, you could deliver significantly higher revenues and performance for your organisation and a better customer experience. Not only that, you could improve your inventory management, which again is better for customers and your bottom line, but you could also improve the performance of your website for customers and build better, clearer data about your customers and more.

For digital shoppers, the primary reason for abandoning an online shopping order was the high extra costs at checkout (shipping being significant), followed by discount codes that do not work, the requirement to set up an account and the process taking too long.[53] [54] Knowing this, it's not surprising that Amazon works hard to promote its Amazon Prime product and has a laser-like focus on shipping costs and ease of checkout.

49 https://www.afr.com/companies/telecommunications/elon-musk-s-starlink-global-internet-creeps-onto-nbn-s-turf-20211221-p59j87.

50 https://www.afr.com/politics/federal/nbn-won-t-ever-earn-commercial-return-former-exec-20221202-p5c3lt.

51 https://www.shopify.com/blog/shopping-cart-abandonment.

52 https://www.shopify.com/blog/shopping-cart-abandonment.

53 https://www.statista.com/statistics/457078/category-cart-abandonment-rate-worldwide/.

54 https://www.shopify.com/blog/shopping-cart-abandonment.

I have worked with companies that have undertaken thorough research on their abandonment rates. In one case a high percentage of potential customers reached the second stage of a three-stage process and then abandoned the cart. So, the right question to ask was: What is it about stage two? Does it ask for too much information? Does it take too long? Do people get stuck filling out the information? By asking numerous questions, changing elements of the process, and using AB testing, the company was able to pinpoint the pain points.

Utilising and analysing data also have the benefit of anonymity of 'observation'. Known as the Hawthorne effect, people behave differently when they know they are being observed. In surveys, there are any number of biases that can creep or leap into play: non-response, response (answering with what someone thinks the survey/interview wants to hear), question design and order, halo effect and more. This said, you are better off observing than not. It is also why looking at data (de-identified credit cards, shopping preferences, subscriptions, memberships etc.) is significantly more accurate because you're not intervening in the customer's behaviour. Rather, you get a raw, objective signal.

Dell knows what customers want as it deals directly with them every moment of every day. Michael Dell would have seen the demand curve for processing capacity go up every minute/day and asked what could be done: What can we build that fits into the next best view of the customer?

Data and attention

Seventy-two per cent of all companies are working on trying to improve customer experience.[55] What is also clear is customers are, in the main, overwhelmed with alternatives and complexity, with choice fatigue developing quite quickly. The scarcest resource today is attention. This in turn has led us to a world where companies that remove customer angst, with easy-to-understand processes and little or zero friction, are winning.

The best customer experience is often not discernible at all, as it is friction-free. When you stream a Netflix TV show it just works. The experience is good, because you don't need to talk, walk, click or chat, it just plays. If you sit still the next episode plays in a friction-free model (which we now know as bingeing). How does your business compare with low-friction competitors?

As new ways of understanding customers evolve, the process of finding them in market while you have their attention for your product or service is key. In a world where customers are always on via social media, carpet bombing of

---

55 https://www.forrester.com/press-newsroom/72-of-businesses-name-improving-customer-experience-their-top-priority/.

emails in our inbox, or streams of interruptions with app updates, prompts, recommendations, makes winning in the attention economy challenging. My son for example turns on ad blockers on all his web services. The only time he turns off the ad blocker is on a site where he cares about the person or product. He allows them to receive some ad revenue or data from him, but it's a conscious choice about who he allows to commercialise his attention.

No one in business can escape from the truth that what you measure matters and that the data and metrics you put in also matter. As Andrew Chen, investor at Andreessen Horowitz, former executive at Uber and author of *The Cold Start Problem: How to Start and Scale Network Effects*, says:

> There are useful metrics, meaningless metrics, misapplied metrics. You can really mess it up here. I've been an advisor to Dropbox kind of off and on over the years and one of the things they did in the early days that I thought was so interesting was that they actually saw themselves as a consumer company. And the reason for that was when they looked inside a Dropbox folder most were full of photos.

What Chen went on to describe was how, although drop box had many customers using it for photo storage and sharing, what a more detailed analysis found was they higher-value users were sharing work flow of spreadsheets, and documents on multiple devices. He made the point that the metrics you measure matter and to make sure your strategy is aligned with real customer metrics that can be measured and analysed, not just counted.[56]

Today, the signals (and noise) of customer behaviour are everywhere. Leaders need to know how to harness and understand the signal. The challenge is to have:

1. The governance in place to ethically capture the customers' signals.
2. The business cases aligned with customer interest in using the customers' signals.
3. Operational effectiveness to deploy the learnings and actions from the customers' signals.
4. The culture in the team is to be innovative with how to create more benefits for the customer that the customer values.

Of course, every company has to start somewhere. To paraphrase Warren Buffett, 'A good idea should scream.' So, I suggest addressing the above points and these questions when anyone talks about data.

---

56 https://a16z.com/book/the-cold-start-problem.

Do you believe that increasing our understanding of our customers is a good idea, on the proviso that you do it in ways that are transparent to our customers as well as legal and ethical?

Do you think the organisation is vulnerable if these actions are not taken? How can the journey start in a way that allows the organisation to hunt and kill a couple of quick assumptions, as that will build up confidence in how data can reveal what customers really want, and what else might they want in the future?

This is the start of your AI: Game On future.

CHAPTER TAKEAWAYS

1. Data collection and customer understanding are essential for success in the intention and attention economy; an ethical framework is mandatory.

2. Innovation and addressing unmet customer needs are key to creating successful products and services.

3. An ethical and innovative organisational culture will add value to the customer experience, particularly in app development, online interactivity and new business models.

4. Effective data use is essential for finding, keeping and understanding customers' needs and optimising towards future customer needs.

5. Companies must predict and adapt to future customer needs to stay relevant in a rapidly changing business landscape as predictive capability is game changing.

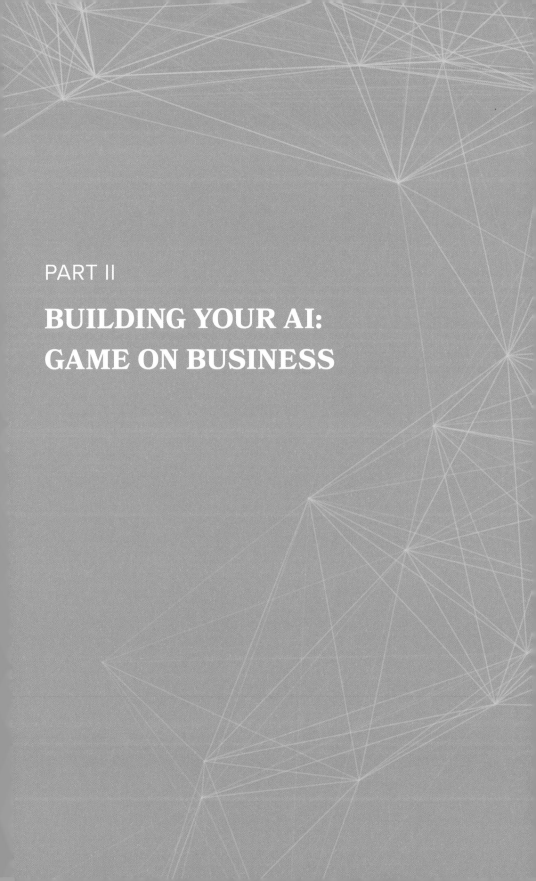

PART II

BUILDING YOUR AI: GAME ON BUSINESS

Chapter 5

THE COMPANY OF TOMORROW, TODAY

'The future is already here – it's just not evenly distributed.'
— William Gibson

Welcome to the machine learning machine, the company of tomorrow

AI: Game On companies will effectively have a data spine, much like the human spine, which supports the moving parts and vital organs, and has the soft tissue of nerves to allow information to flow around and through the entire system and back to the decision-making brain.

BOARD DECISIONS SUPPORTED BY DATA

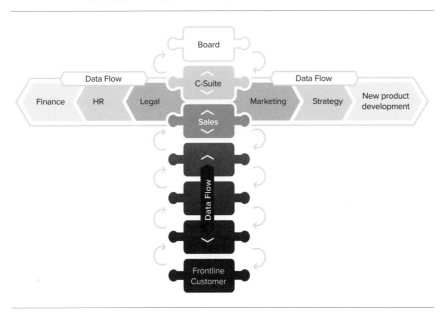

In data science, it is now widely understood that the best data will beat the best analytics. You can have the best weather forecaster on earth looking out a window and when you line up their forecasting power to hundreds of satellites in real time, you get the point.

The 'whole organisation' use of data and AI deployment is already embedded in the tech giants Tesla, Meta, Google, Amazon, Alibaba, Tencent, Netflix and others. There are even a few companies that have AI on their board with a valid vote on key policy matters!

In 2014, Deep Knowledge Ventures, a Hong Kong venture-capital firm specialising in regenerative medicine, announced that it had appointed an algorithm named VITAL to its board. VITAL allegedly makes investment recommendations by analysing huge amounts of data regarding the financial situation, clinical trials and intellectual property of prospective companies. Like the other five board members VITAL gets to vote on whether the company makes an investment.

There is some early evidence that the new AI tools will create more job losses in white-collar work than blue-collar. Machines are much closer to doing the work in the back end of finance and HR than they are at painting the warehouse. As AI advances in every aspect of corporate life, we must ask what does the boardroom of 20 years from now look like? What skills will be needed to govern in a world of mass adoption of AI?

Salesforce CEO Marc Benioff utilises data-driven analysis through an unreleased version of the company's AI product, Einstein, to help him make better decisions. Einstein accompanies him to the Monday morning staff meeting where Salesforce's top executives meet and discuss different regions, products and opportunities. Then Benioff asks one other executive for their opinion. That executive is Einstein, the AI machine. Benioff claims, 'Einstein comes without bias.' So, because it's just based on the data, it's a very exciting next-generation tool that he says has transformed him as a CEO.[57]

Sure, these are early outlying use cases but there will be more over time, as AI capability grows and human capability is limited by the constraints of our capacity to consider, interpret and synthesise vast amounts of information.

> 'Without data you're just another person with an opinion.'
> — W. Edwards Deming, data scientist

In the recent past the first data and AI iterations were mostly and understandably focused on marketing optimisation, churn models and the like. This was

---

57   https://www.govenda.com/blog/artificial-intelligence-in-corporate-governance/.

and is a good early use case for data and AI that has had material impacts on profit. The journey started here in part because it's where the data is easiest to gather. The digital targeting of media has advanced faster than logistic optimisation, procurement or HR analytics. Many of the smartest minds in the world have captured the power of data to harness the billions spent on advertising. This focus has propelled Alphabet, Meta Platforms, Amazon and Apple to the top of Fortune 500 companies over the past 15 years.[58]

These companies and thousands of others are utilising and constantly growing rich data sets, and there's a whole ecosystem of adtech and martech flowing around this. Data and AI have now moved into all the other myriad functions of the enterprise – logistics and supply chains, rents, procurement, allocation of capital, and maintenance.

However, when it comes to understanding your staff's needs, who needs support, who should have the promotion and why, it is a different story. By comparison, the people analytics industry is where media was in the 1990s. It's game on in the people management sector and AI and data will change the way we hire and remunerate employees. Data and AI will also change how companies engage with contractors, gig workers, consultants, software suppliers, lawyers, accountants, insurance providers, fund managers and more. Data science in the HR department is just getting started.

Machine learning operations (MLOps) are transforming how data and AI are being deployed in business. Companies that are harnessing MLOps have already shifted gears from exploring what AI can do via experimental pilot projects on the sidelines or in specific silos within their business to creating a standard, company-wide AI factory capable of achieving scale and value with speed and efficiency. MLOps take advantage of massive improvements in AI tooling, workflows, open software solutions, modular options and platforms.

AI: Game On companies are leveraging their data to drive margin and market share, nurturing it as a strategic asset and applying it in ways that have a concrete impact on their business. Think of Atlassian and Canva, as great Australian examples. John Deere, the 180-year-old manufacturer of farming and industrial machinery, is also harnessing data and machine learning. With its See & Spray technology, high-resolution cameras capture 20 images per second. Based on the images and artificial intelligence, the system recognises the difference between cultivated plants and weeds so that individual plants can be specifically treated. With this new generation of weed control, the use of pesticides can be reduced by up to 80–90%.[59]

---

58 https://www.statista.com/statistics/263264/top-companies-in-the-world-by-market-capitalization/.

59 https://digital.hbs.edu/platform-digit/submission/john-deere-killing-weeds-precisely-with-see-spray-technology/.

Despite all the evidence, discussion and success of data/AI-native businesses, why is it that so many companies are yet to harness the full potential of their data? A 2022 State of Data Culture Report noted that 97% of data leaders said their companies had suffered the consequences of ignoring data, from missing out on new revenue opportunities, poorly forecasting performance and making bad investments.[60] Any one of these could be business-ending; all three will almost certainly result in the demise or takeover of an organisation.

What can be done to enable this change and do it fast?

Shifting from data ownership to customer benefit – the importance of thoughtful data use

The human body is remarkable in its capacity to measure what is going on around it. Our five senses are plugged into the largest, most effective brain anywhere in the known universe at the time of writing. We are also a machine that can be distracted in an instant.

The human 'flight, fight or freeze' response is part of how the brain runs a prediction on what it expects to happen and gears us up for its prediction. If you put the kettle on, like you do four times a day, and this time it explodes, that is counter to the predictive model your brain had of the kettle's next move. The shock will be out of sequence with the expectation and your consciousness will be acutely focused on the disparity between the prediction and the new reality. Full attention will be on at this moment.

Deciding what to pay attention to in daily life is not that different to deciding what to pay attention to in a business. You can chase a lot of small issues like the noise of the fan in your computer, or you can focus your energy on that life-changing new initiative for your well-being.

The human body, with the five senses operating well, and a brain that is functioning reasonably well, has all it needs for most of what comes our way. Organisations are not born with those systems in place. They have to be created, designed and orchestrated to deliver 'what good looks like'.

Previously, most companies were organised in a top-down hierarchical structure with clearly defined departments (silos/empires), prescriptive job descriptions, and rigid reporting lines. Information (data) was collated for specific responses (orders, invoicing, supply purchases, employee payments etc.) with separate specific corporate service areas: legal, accounting, advertising, marketing and so on. Information was contained and passed through 'lochs' in carefully calibrated releases.

---

60 https://www.alation.com/blog/data-culture-gap-report/.

If you decide to do only one thing with data, do this: set it up to allow you to understand what your customer feels when using your product. Build systems that allow you to deeply recognise what your customer feels. If your customers are waiting hours to connect with a call centre, and you're not measuring that, you are toast. If your website checkout is not easy, it's over – you just don't know it yet. If the delivery of a customer's order is not made on time, or at all, you've lost the game. If you're not nurturing a relationship with your customers, they'll leave you to find someone who will.

Your customers are one click away from someone who can make their life easier, better, faster, cheaper, make them feel more appreciated or all of these things

More critically, if you're tracking and measuring the wrong things you could be responding to the wrong signals. Organisations can choose to notice the loudest voice, the outlier, or the oddball on Twitter banging on about some passion project of theirs, and why your organisation is not acting on it. Or you can focus on what loyal customers expect from you next, and that is a prediction you can make that will pay dividends fast. You can put all your attention focusing on the one complaint (the noise) from the outlier on Twitter, or you can notice the 95% of customers who, through their often-silent observable behaviours, have given you strong signals about what they like about your company and clues about how to improve it.

As a board member, CEO or executive, it's important to enable data and AI throughout the business through a data-led culture. If you're in a legacy company there may be material benefits to loosen firmly rooted, siloed ways of working, to open up the data lochs and get the data flowing. Of course, data guard rails, privacy and ethics need to be your North Star.

It is leadership that is needed to help, to set the aspirations for the company, to facilitate shared goals, ensure accountability and invest in the talent and resources to make it happen. Anchor the initiatives from the customer's perspective. John Deere's innovation about using AI to spot weeds, and to apply a small amount of herbicide precisely on this weed, is good for the customer, and better for the planet. It is also harder to clone than a normal tractor and their competitors will need to respond or be seen as last year's model. If you happen to be in the business of selling herbicide this is a threat from outside your traditional competitive set.

Telco companies are awash with data. They know where we are, what cell tower is connected to each device, who we call, when, for how long, who we text, when and where we work out, who we cohabitate with, who we are friends with via the location of our phones and people we spend time with at the same locations. For sound privacy reasons, telcos don't use this information unless the law requires it (think the police, homeland security, ICAC, ASIC, the courts and more).

A business colleague of mine who lives in the UK was overseas when a caller (a thief) rang their telco to say they wanted to port (move) their number to a new phone. The telco obliged, never asking for the password that was on the account; they just happily ported the mobile number. As soon as the transfer occurred the actual owner's phone stopped working. Oblivious to what had occurred, he called his telco to say his phone was not working. The telco never mentioned that they ported the mobile number moments before but did helpfully advise that the bill was up to date and there should be no issues. The call centre was not linked to the systems in the porting department, so they were blind to this issue. Offering comfort, the telco representative reassuringly said that 'it should sort itself out, our system here shows it's all in order.' Things were not in order. The CEO of this telco is on the regular speaking circuit recounting their AI prowess and customer-centricity credentials, seemingly oblivious to the pain and knock-on effects created by their lack of customer understanding due to their poor technology systems. The lack of sound data hygiene inflicts massive damage on customers, and hundreds of millions in cybercrime that is being borne by banks.

Over the next eight minutes the hacker used the mobile number to ask for new passwords for banking apps and ran off with the equivalent of $400,000 from two banks (both of which purport to have high-grade AI-predicting capability). If you call your bank from your mobile number their systems will assume largely it is you calling. If you open their banking apps with your mobile and reset the passwords these are sent via text to your phone, as two-factor identification is seen as best practice, which is simply not true when a phone number is ported. Once your phone is hacked, all these credentials are moved to the thief and it is game over.

When you pause to think of the data the telco has, it is incredible that this whole saga can occur, and that they ignore the data that can help the customer.

The fraudster tested the banks further, changing the home address linked to one account just for good measure, from a high-value home in a wealthy part of the city to a significantly lower value area, even though the bank had a mortgage on the home. Surely this would have set off a potential hack alert. No such luck. My friend even had a private banker at this leading bank, who would have instantly known that this change was fraud, but alas their brilliant AI-enabled systems snoozed through the crimes.

It took my friend two months to unravel the hack and another two months to sort out the reimbursement of the stolen funds! All because the data systems of the telco and bank were simply not up to standard and the thieves know this. Meanwhile, the cybercriminals sail away on their mega yachts in the South of France.

And where are the telco and bank boards? This is enabling large-scale crime, and we see yet again how data is too important to be left to the data department.

A director of one of the leading banks in Australia said to me this sort of crime is costing her bank around $500 million a year. At this loss, close to $10 million a week, the payback from building systems that protect the customer and the bank seems to be a no-brainer.

Credit card companies are much better at deploying and using global, large-scale analytics at scale and have developed some good predictive AI. For example, if you fill up a tank of petrol at 9:06 am in one area and try to buy a pair of shoes 50 kilometres away at 9:15 am, their systems will automatically flag this as a fraud, as you can't have travelled that far in 9 minutes. They also have a flag on the card to indicate if the card was presented or not presented. These and other more sophisticated data analytics systems are built in to protect their customers first and foremost and have the additional benefit of reducing the cost of refunding clients for fraudulent transactions. Banks are working on many initiatives to reduce this sort of crime, but an honest assessment of their real capability and board-level risk analysis is needed. In the last few months some of the banks, some using telco data, have made powerful corrective steps to combat some of this fraud. There are still mountains to be climbed here, and a vast societal benefit from use of AI and data to stop fraud.

Data's power to hunt and kill assumptions

There's a tendency in humans to invent an explanation when they don't have the data to really understand the issues. Meteorites were signs of the gods, the eclipse of the moon was a miracle, not a predicable event based on maths. Organisations have myths too when there is a void of data. One of the jobs to be done everywhere in corporate life, especially at the board and executive level, is to empower their organisations and employees to hunt and kill assumptions.

What is your organisation sure of that may not be true? It is a good idea to ask yourself and colleagues what your own organisation's myths are that are yet to be tested by data.

Ben Ashton, a friend of mine and former colleague at Quantium, is a smart lawyer and now CEO of CommBank iQ.[61] Ben and I first worked at PBL after which he was CEO of an in-home tech support business. They ran a field service team of a few hundred people visiting people in their homes. Back in 2010, Quantium was looking for early customers to test case their data services so I went to see Ben. I asked him about his customers: their age, educational background, spending habits, suburbs, occupation, income and so on. Ben asked his field force to report back on these metrics from their interactions with customers. The results came back stating that his customers were predominantly 35–45, high-income men from upper-income suburbs.

We then ran the bank data (in a de-identified privacy-compliant way). The majority of Ben's customers were 55+, in middle-income areas. Ben's first reaction was that the data couldn't be right, so we retested it. It was right. Ben was surprised but it did help to explain why his marketing efforts weren't getting the traction they should, and it explained his feeling of pushing against a headwind or current. How could his field force not know their own customers?

The answer is simple. Most of us want to believe our customers are like us and if you're a successful marketing executive, salesperson or product development person, you could well prefer the idea that your customers are a bit like you, or someone you aspire to be like. It's a classic example of unconscious bias and we all have it. Real customer data when carefully used can have far less bias.

The silent voice of the real customer needs to be heard and understood. If that conflicts with what your team believes, that is good. Busting myths may not make you friends but it will help the business in the longer term.

When I joined the board of the NRMA (Australia's largest motoring and tourism mutual) there was a long-standing belief that the most loyal customers were the ones who occasionally broke down, used the legendary roadside assistance to great peace of mind, then went on their way, happy with the service. The NRMA has a very high net promoter score (NPS) of 82. This customer was often thought to be a young mother with kids who felt vulnerable on the side of the road, so joined to feel safe. They were loyal customers and it all made perfect sense. Then we did some work on the data.

The team ran the data on the most loyal customers, to evaluate their breakdown rates versus other customers. How long was the wait time when they broke

---

61   https://quantium.com/commbank-iq/.

down? What was the resolution in the field? Once we had the data it was clear that the most loyal customers weren't breaking down very often at all. It was an assumption.

The data told us that the most loyal customers use some of the NRMA's other services. So, it's the other services that are very much helping to add value to customers' own sense of value and belonging, as well as the great roadside assistance work. Once we saw the data, the objective evidence, we asked more questions of the data. What other services do they use, how often, when? What other services are they interested in that we might be able to provide in the future? What can we predict about their needs? How can we know them better to serve them better?

These and other insights led us to build a new strategy around tourism and we have moved a significant part of our balance sheet as a consequence.

This is data impacting the strategy and strategy impacting data. When the balance sheets are more aligned with the customers' needs, the company is moving with its customers' needs and emerging needs. The board is also informed through the data to help govern for the future.

Apple captured the watch market at breakneck speed. The Apple Watch was released in April 2015 with 4.2 million sold in the first quarter. By December 2020 there were 110 million Apple Watches in circulation.[62] It took Apple only four years to outpace the entire Swiss watch market, with Strategic Analytics claiming Apple shipped 30.7 million units of smartwatches worldwide in 2019 compared to 21.1 million for all Swiss watch brands combined. The use cases on the Apple Watch are near endless. The use case on the Swiss watch is largely unchanged; that is, it tells me the time.

Threat of substitution

Substitution of products and services is significantly impacted by data, AI and machine learning.

If you have an Apple Watch, it's likely that you've got another Apple product, perhaps an iPhone, iPad, MacBook, HomePod, Apple TV or Apple Music. You might also have connected your Spotify account and fitness apps, and you speak to Siri. However, changing your phone to a Samsung or another Android phone is not as straightforward as it appears, as there are all sorts of interoperability issues that make an ongoing relationship with Apple more likely, or stickier. The cost of switching your phone is now significantly higher than it was before Apple entered the market. Remember Blackberry?

---

62 https://en.wikipedia.org/wiki/Apple_Watch.

You don't need to own an iPhone; you can have any mobile phone, Samsung, Google Pixel, TCL, OPPO, Xiaomi and more. You can find a mobile phone that's 90% cheaper than the iPhone. Millions of people are fiercely loyal to their iPhone, camping out the night before new versions are released. Loyalty is reinforced by data and AI networking, linked product apps in Apple's case. That's one reason why Apple is worth so much money, because changing is hard and very few Apple customers want to change. If you have all your photos in your phone and iCloud, shared across your devices, you've got all your apps to access everything seamlessly. Apple is a lifestyle enabler.

Tesla is similar. If you own a Tesla, they have all your driving information and you're part of a Tesla ecosystem. You have various navigational, driving, charging station apps connected to your car and your phone. You might also have taken out insurance and received a discount, as Tesla is able to provide detailed information about how you use your car, how you drive it, where you drive it and more. Tesla is starting to market its own insurance.[63] Changing a car is now also linked to data use as you lose all your data with it.

What Apple and Tesla have in common is that they have real fans, and are good at delighting their customers. Have you ever heard anyone talk about their insurance company the way they talk about their Tesla? Can you honestly say your company or organisation does that?

CHAPTER TAKEAWAYS

1. Data is the spine of future-facing companies, and the best data wins over the best analytics. When the best data meets the best analytics, the organisation is very hard to beat.

2. Major tech companies have already embedded AI in their operations, giving them a big advantage, but AI-based tools are also spreading into other sectors.

3. Data and AI are changing the way we hire and remunerate employees, and machine learning operations (MLOps) are transforming the deployment of AI in businesses.

4. Protecting customer data is crucial, and organisations should rely on data, not assumptions, to understand their customers.

5. Real customer insight can be obtained through analysing real customer data, and businesses must be careful not to rely on flawed assumptions about their customers.

---

63 https://www.tesla.com/en_AU/insurance.

Chapter 6

NAVIGATING THE DECISION-MAKING REVOLUTION, DECISION AS A SERVICE, DAAS

'If we have data, let's look at data. If all we have are opinions, let's go with mine.' – Jim Barksdale, former president and CEO of Netscape, founder of Barksdale Group

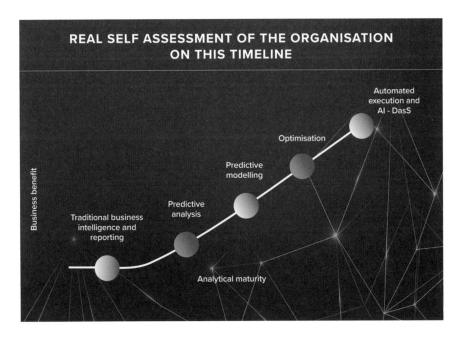

People make thousands of micro-decisions each day. Cornell University research found that people make an average of 226 decisions each day on food alone.[64] Being a CEO is a particularly taxing role. Management was described

---

64   Wansink and Sobal, 2007.

in my MBA textbook years ago as 'sitting in a stream of interruptions', and most interruptions need a decision.

Yet for all the high cognitive load of running a business, think about this. One of the algorithms I have seen deployed in retail has 23 trillion variables and makes millions of decisions each second. These then move into recommendations for customers, and actions for management and staff. We are in a decision-making revolution – welcome to decisions as a service (DaaS).

Car insurance companies are sitting on millions of individuals' claims history, all tagged with when, where, who, what, how, and often why the accident occurred – all key data points on accidents. Are men aged 29 driving a white Subaru on a Friday night at more risk than the same-aged male driving a Corolla? They know. It's in the data. What is the most dangerous time of day to travel to the beach? They know, and on it goes. Insurers are in the box seat to innovate in a way that their customers would value and which would drive profits through lower claims. Yet they can't because the data is locked up on a one-way bet that calculates a price risk against their customers. The result is that it is causing frustration instead of being liberated to help their customers.

> **'Risk comes from not knowing what you're doing.'**
> – Warren Buffett

A relative of mine was in a car crash recently. Not hurt thankfully, and they were not at fault. My relative took a photo of the damage to both cars and obtained the number plate and name of the driver. A good result in the circumstances as the other driver was not very cooperative.

She sent through the claim to her insurance company expecting it to be paid. The insurance company (a top-tier multibillion-dollar entity) rejected the claim, saying they needed to have the address of the at-fault driver and that without this information the claim would be rejected. My relative googled the person, found their place of work and address, offered this along with the photos, and the name of the witness who was prepared to go to court if needed to state the other driver was at fault. The insurance company again said that without the home address of the other driver the claim would be denied. My relative rebutted this, exasperated but noting that privacy laws mean that they are not meant to stalk the at-fault to obtain the home address. Surely the number plate and the insurance companies' resources to track them down should be enough. The insurance company was adamant it was her responsibility to find the home address of the at-fault driver, so I suggested she pose the insurance company this question, as they have a large market share: 'Is it possible that this number plate and name I have is insured by you?' The call centre person typed the details into the server and bingo!

They knew this customer and the illusive home address of the at-fault driver was on their database! However, this is not all fixed.

This should have shown up as the claim was presented, and negated 11 frustrated calls to the company. The same insurance company CEO talks at the AGM about their systems being the most advanced using algorithms and AI, saying how they knew great details about their customer claims, preferences and risk profiles. There are PR pieces from them claiming in effect 'we use AI, machine learning to process our claims and automate the processes for our customers at real scale and in real time'. As is so often the case, when the C-suite thinks the problem is solved that problem multiplies as the organisation has lost sight of what it's like to be a customer. In a fully AI: Game On world this whole process will look very different. Crash detection could grab dash cam footage and apply for your insurance claim in close to real time, while your AI-enabled bot fills out the forms and asks you to cross-check before it sends it off with your proof of what happened.

'It impossible for a man to learn what he thinks he already knows.'
— Epictetus

Tesla is now offering car insurance based on your own real driving behaviours that are of course detected in the Tesla. At the time of writing, Tesla insurance is growing to 12 states in the USA. Their website says the process to activate the insurance will be one minute, so contrast that with your current insurance forms. We are seeing the 'the organisation with the best use of customer data win again'. My sense is that all car companies, as they become much more data-driven, will move to use their own customers' real driving risks to offer insurance. Instead of a team of actuaries trying to model out my driving risks, the car knows. It knows how far I drive, when, where, how I brake, how I accelerate, even near misses will be shown in a Tesla, and any impact will be captured through on-board cameras. Better data wins again, and if you are running a car insurance company, this is now a real challenge. Tesla is reaching into a multibillion-dollar industry adjacent to their core business, and leading with customer benefits and better data, a very powerful combination.

MIT's Computer Science and Artificial Intelligence Laboratory (CSAIL) and the Qatar Centre for Artificial Intelligence have developed a deep learning model that predicts very high-resolution crash risk maps.[65] Fed on a combination of historical crash data, road maps, satellite imagery and GPS traces, the risk maps describe the expected number of crashes over a period of time in the future, to identify high-risk areas and predict future crashes. Insurance

---

65 https://openaccess.thecvf.com/content/ICCV2021/papers/He_Inferring_High-Resolution_
Traffic_Accident_Risk_Maps_Based_on_Satellite_Imagery_ICCV_2021_paper.pdf.

companies could access these maps and make them available to their customers as part of really helping their customers. To my knowledge, they don't do this for their customers.

At a meeting I had at Microsoft in Seattle a few years ago, I was shown an AI application that had mapped US road fatalities, with the known data of the tragic incidents, plotting weather, car type, location, time of day and any other information that was available. The use of their AI was powerful. This sort of information can be used to help people lower their own personal driving risks.

In one lifetime we have changed from human-only decisions to decisions informed by data and AI. Today we are seeing decisions as a service (DaaS) at the frontier of AI, with machines that can start to understand complex patterns, processes and concepts, and that can create new algorithms to seek out new patterns. They are increasingly self-adapting and self-learning.

Data and AI have changed the way humans and, therefore, businesses can make decisions. At the heart of this is genuine human-machine interaction. What can data and AI help us with? What questions could and should businesses be asked and be able to answer? What should we turn our attention to and focus on? How do businesses decide who or what decides? How will your organisation think through what decisions you will delegate to machines and what will be the oversight of AI-generated decisions?

AI is the first plausible challenge to human supremacy in thought. At the time of writing, there is no real consensus that we are about to have artificial general intelligence, AGI, in the immediate future that will take over human life. It is for now our subservient tool, albeit with rapidly growing capability and not without the need for regulation and guard rails. The likes of Elon Musk have some concerning views on what AGI could do over time and how it is possible to imagine a world where poor controls over the use of AGI could create catastrophic implications. I will not drift into over-the-horizon speculation: I will leave that for others.

What is not fictitious is that right now, for the first time, we are at a point where humans have viable emerging competition for our concept of being the most intelligent 'apparatus' on the planet. Human brains evolve very slowly, while AI is bounding, compounding and self-adapting. ChatGPT and the spawning of many other AI tools are rapidly evolving and being discovered by millions of people for their capacity to write, draw and create. There are bugs, it's not perfect by a long way; however, it and other systems are very likely to improve quickly, and won't get tired at night, won't suffer eye strain, they will just keep working. Jasper and Andi search (disclosure: I'm an investor and advisor) are good examples of new businesses leveraging new AI applications. There will be many more and the pace of acceleration is very likely to increase from here.

The potential for large language models (LLMs) to help us, and also confuse and abuse our trust, is large. If done well it's a boon for human productivity. If done badly, or worse, aimed at disrupting society, the impact could be staggering. LLMs can be customised to help or be optimised for spreading misinformation.

Deciding how AI is deployed, governed and aligned with human dignity is the decision of our time and of future generations. And by 'our' I mean business leaders, directors and executives, medical researchers, regulators and ethicists as we are at the forefront (or should be) of implementing AI into our business models, medical research, laws and regulation, and global systems of finance and commerce.

The decision-making revolution comes with great responsibility and we've seen how far behind national and global regulation has been, in many instances, in the data and AI race. While it might seem governments are now aware of the challenges, they are playing catch up with the global data/AI-enabled companies that are still leaping ahead.

The major technology firms are racing ahead in AI development and deployment and putting application into the population at pace and without a full understanding of what the AI impacts are or could be. We would not allow this in medicine, food production or motor vehicles.

Boards need to work on this at the governance level, and as mentioned before governance derives from the Latin word *gubernare* meaning 'to steer'. Standing on the bridge of a ship gives a higher perspective for navigation. A crow's nest higher, satellites higher still. Data use at scale allows a wider perspective. The aperture is opened. At the same time businesses need both telescopes and microscopes (literally and figuratively) to understand markets, their customers' behaviour, the patterns of product or service use and at both the macro level on the horizon, and the subatomic data level for each interaction. Great data use cases allow for perspective of scale, and atomic-level detail for personalisation. Netflix sees macro trends in content and micro use of the customer all through the same data-driven system. They can commission new shows at lower risk than traditional content makers as they can predict which customers will watch the new show. Not focus groups; real, scaled insights.

History in some ways could be described as the study of surprises; it is the arrival of large-scale events that were not well predicted. If the assassination of JFK was predicted on that day in Dallas the car would not have driven in front of the sniper. History noted it was a tragic surprise event. Surprises happen from a lack of data or a misunderstanding of available information or inability to predict what is going to happen next.

The late Henry Kissinger, in the book he recently co-authored with Eric Schmidt and Peter Huttenlocher, *The Age of AI*, makes the point that often when something is not understandable by humans, they perceive it as an act of God, bad luck or nature. More precisely, it's also a lack of data and insight from data. Earth-quakes can appear to be random; however, we are increasingly able to predict when and where they will occur with better sensors, data and models, even though we still have a way to go. We can certainly better predict the flow-on effects of earthquakes such as tsunamis and ash fallout.

So, it's important to understand how the signal from the front line in so many organisations gets blocked and can't make its way to the boardroom. What is the gunk in the information flow that kills empires? Who in the organisation has a vested interest in messing with the signal? How can you spot this in your organisation? Better still, how can you create a system that delivers this information directly to the leadership team with no interference? That is what an AI: Game On company can do.

What your customer wants next from you is a question that holds incredible value if you can answer it well, and before your competition does. Deciding what actions to take or not take, which allows you to understand what the customer needs, is the key asset in the intention/attention economy. Google's empire is built on harvesting this signal and auctioning the results at close to the speed of light.

Kevin Kelly, in his thoughtful book *The Inevitable*, says abundant answers simply generate more questions. 'While the machine can expand answers indefinitely, our time to form the next question is very limited. When answers become cheap and questions become valuable.'[66] This is going to be part of the role of the boardroom for AI: Game On.

> **'If I had an hour to solve a problem and my life depended on**
> **it I would use the first 55 minutes determining the questions to ask,**
> **for once I know the proper question I could solve the problem in**
> **less than 5 minutes.'** – Einstein

Good questions will be created by machines but for the moment it's largely a human challenge. Perhaps the future of AI is more about how fast AI learns what are the best questions to ask. There are some early tools here that do prompt human questions to ask.

Attention of organisations needs to go to what are the great questions and how can these be answered with data and AI that changes the trajectory of the business. Michael Lewis's book *The Premonition* speaks to the story of Dr Jose,

---

66   The Inevitable, Kevin Kelly, Viking, 2016.

who had trained at Harvard and spent a decade researching disease at the National Institute of Health. He was a genius at figuring out what was wrong with patients and at training young doctors. Each morning, he spent genuine, intimate time with patients, listening to their stories/memories of what they'd been up to. Through the conversation he was digging into the patient's life and through this information he formed a differential diagnosis of the infectious diseases that might have caused the symptoms or as Dr Jose put it, 'What have you been doing that puts you at risk for whatever the hell you've got?'

A college student turned up one day with a dramatic and mysterious rash on his torso and when Dr Jose arrived, he let the student share a tour of his social life and asked, 'When was the last time you were in a hot tub?' Not, 'Were you ever in a hot tub?' The kid's response: 'A few days ago.' 'Anyone with you?' Dr Jose. 'Yeah, a few friends.' 'Any of them have a rash?' he asked. 'Actually, yes. My roommate does, just not as bad.' It was classic Pseudomonas bacteria you can get from hot tubs. In medical school, doctors are shown how to follow a checklist to get the life history of a new patient, not to explore the patient's social relationships. Communicable diseases require a different approach as they are spread by person-to-person contact. Asking the right questions is vital in medicine as it is in boardrooms.

As Sam Harris comments, 'Human beings are opinion machines.'[67] It's true we are wired to have opinions on everything. The old quote 'Often wrong but never in doubt' can be applied to so many instances in human endeavour. Changing our minds when we are presented with new data is not a slam dunk either. There is significant research that shows just how hard it is for us to overcome what we previously believed in the face of new contrary information, commonly referred to as a believed perspective. Conceptual conservatism is maintaining a belief despite new information that firmly contradicts it. Just look at the worldwide reaction by some groups to the facts of Covid. Add to this the backfire effect: where beliefs may be strengthened when others present evidence debunking them. Of course, the echo chambers of social media, in relation to Covid-19, act to magnify belief systems as algorithms feed people what they know they like and want to read/see/hear. Many of the new AI tools are not correcting this, as they too will play back plenty of well-written mis-information.

I have been in many conversations with C-suite and board members over recent years where they ask, 'How can we become more customer-driven, more in tune with the needs of the customer?' I find myself saying this in response: 'You can't fix what you can't understand', and the trouble is most companies just don't have the tools, culture and drive to really understand customers and therefore don't really understand their needs.

---

67   https://www.samharris.org/podcasts.

If you bring enough data to any question, the answer can change a lot and that can inspire the next key question.

What decisions can/should data and AI be applied to?

We're moving from software as a service (SaaS) to an era of decisions as a service (DaaS). It is now possible to automate stupidity.

Sometimes data becomes artificial incompetence. Data applications should be smart, customer-friendly and in the best interests of the customers. Not all are.

There's the disastrous story of United Airlines security staff dragging a passenger off a flight with force as the automated passenger load system had overbooked the flight, a standard practice in the USA and Europe. The passenger on UA Flight 3411 suffered concussion, a broken nose and lost two teeth.[68] A video of the incident went viral costing the airline untold reputational damage; its stock price fell and they were forced to provide a settlement. The airline's staff should have been trained on how to deal with the occurrence and intervene in an appropriate way. The algorithm 'told them to get this passenger off the plane'; however, their systems are not good enough to avoid over-booking, which was the real issue. The system is optimised to maximise revenue, but its capacity to look after customers was found lacking big time.

When considering the interaction between AI and humans in decision-making it is important to understand both the decision-making process and the types of decisions that are typically made.

The OODA loop (observe, orient, decide, act) is used to try to help fighter pilots 'outthink' their adversaries.[69] Importantly, it was understood that the pilot would never have 100% of the information they wanted; it was more focused on how much information is acceptable before moving forward.

In addition, in an AI setting, the loop is repeating constantly, and each part is feeding into all the steps simultaneously.

---

68 https://www.washingtonpost.com/transportation/2019/04/09/doctor-who-was-dragged-screaming-united-airlines-flight-finally-breaks-silence/.

69 https://www.businessinsider.com.au/ooda-loop-decision-making-2017-8.

THE AI OODA LOOP

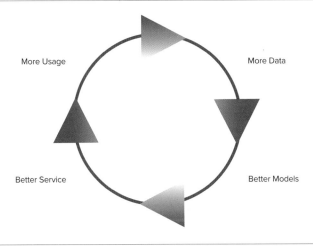

More Usage

More Data

Better Service

Better Models

Now this technique has been co-opted by those wanting to propel business advantages and new business models using data and AI.[70] The OODA loop for AI updates the language, but the intent is just the same.

The more data you have, the better your models get. The better your models are, the better your product/service becomes. This leads to more usage and, subsequently, more data and the cycle continues. Feedback is constant and has to have oversight and considered interpretation by humans.

The more times a business operates through a cycle, the greater the competitive distance. Companies that can and have operationalised this model are going to be harder to catch up with. Amazon's flywheel is a much-cited story about how the more they create value for customers the better they can help them next time. Tesla information about road conditions is growing fast and creates better driving conditions for their customers. The data of the customer when captured and used by them, for them, is a powerful flywheel effect.

Types of decisions

As with other business areas, the types of decisions executives and boards need to make in relation to their data and AI operations fall into two main categories. Strategic (Type 1) decisions are consequential, irreversible or extremely difficult to reverse. They are one-way doors and must be made methodically, deliberately, slowly and with great consideration. Selling the

---

70 https://venturebeat.com/2021/09/19/want-to-win-with-ai-focus-on-your-leadership-not-the-competition/.

family home is one such decision. Non-strategic (Type 2) decisions are changeable and reversible. These can and should be made quickly by a high-judgement individual or small team. Interestingly Jeff Bezos addressed this very issue in his 1997 shareholders letter noting that as companies get bigger there is a tendency to make the processes around Type 2 decisions the same as Type 1 decisions, which slows down innovation to customer needs.

The governance framework of how to use AI, and to ensure that customer sanctity and ethics apply (see Chapter 8), is a strategic Type 1 decision. The ongoing data operations that feed into AI operation can then become a Type 2 decision if the guard rails are in place, and the governance, in order to do no harm. The delegation of deciding how to decide, who or what decides, is critical. Reviews of all decision-making by AI need to be done to ensure ethical considerations are not subject to drift in goal alignment.

Data can and does work well with strategic and non-strategic decision-making. I saw an M&A transaction that was data-led. The company wanted to expand, and instead of finding targets based on traditional means of engaging investment bankers to identify potential targets, the data found the target company in the behaviours of the customers. To be specific, we found that what the customers of company A were buying was in adjacent categories to the target company B, which was available for acquisition. It was about following the customer to identify the new venture rather than following the investment bank's recommendation from a list of the usual suspects.

While data and AI can and should be utilised throughout an organisation's decision-making processes, even at board level, it's currently most powerful and effective in high-frequency decisions like what offer to make next to customers. Share trading is one obvious place, where the algo-traders are using billions of signals to try to find alpha in the data flows. Approximately 60–73% of all trading in US equities is done by algorithms.[71]

Another example of strategic decision-making in the medical field can be seen in the area of structural biology. Determining the 3D shapes of biological molecules is one of the hardest problems in modern biology and medical discovery. 'Using clever, new machine learning techniques, Stanford University PhD students Stephan Eismann and Raphael Townshend, under the guidance of Ron Dror, associate professor of computer science, have developed an approach that overcomes this problem by predicting accurate structures computationally.'[72]

Of relevance to our decision-making discussions is that instead of specifying what makes a structural prediction more or less accurate, the researchers let

---

71 https://analyzingalpha.com/algorithmic-trading-statistics.

72 https://phys.org/news/2021-08-ai-algorithm-biology.html.

the algorithm discover these molecular features for itself. They did this because they found that the conventional technique of providing such knowledge can sway an algorithm in favour of certain features, thus preventing it from finding other informative features. They took a strategic decision to let the AI decide. The result was impressive:

'The network learned to find fundamental concepts that are key to molecular structure formation, but without explicitly being told to,' said one of the researchers. The exciting aspect is that the algorithm has clearly recovered things that we knew were important, but it has also discovered characteristics that we didn't know about before.[73]

The decision of our time is how to decide who or what decides

Dealing with this challenge will be integral to your organisation's move to AI: Game On and your destiny.

How will you know where AI was used in Type 2 decisions? Who signed off on it? Will a regulator want to understand what's in the decision as a service? What is the source data? Is it verified? What is the customer outcome, and what second- or third-order consequences are there?

What is your defensive moat?

Even if you adopt a real AI strategy, many others will do the same and have access to the same tools and perhaps even the same data. The answer and the advantage will be in the use case. Whoever gets to the customer first with the superior use case starts the new flywheel of scale data use.

Humanity is on a journey that is allowing us to put more and more decisions and actions into the hand of machines. Years ago department stores had a lift driver because passengers were nervous about being in the lift without one. We grow more accustomed to machines making decisions for us every day. Driverless trains were introduced in Japan in the 1980s, then in France and now around the world. The spread of driverless trains is a good reminder that 'new' automated decision-making capability is quickly accepted by people so long as trust and security are not compromised.

Google is a decision as a service (DaaS) pioneer where the value exchange it offers could be summarised as you allow Google to track what you search for, and it uses the intention data so advertisers can target you for a large commercial gain in it in Google's favour. John L. Hennessy, the chairman of parent company Alphabet, told CNBC that Google was hesitant to use its Bard AI in a

---

73   https://phys.org/news/2021-08-ai-algorithm-biology.html.

product as it wasn't 'really ready', and yet Google unveiled its Bard AI in February 2023 amid intense interest in competitor ChatGPT. A promotion for Google Bard featured a factual error — and Alphabet's stock dropped 9% in a day after the mistake received media attention. That was a valuation hit of over $100 billion dollars at the time. If the data giants can get this wrong, it is a lesson that there is real complexity here to be solved and governance needed at board level.

Some consumers don't want to engage in this value exchange, and that should be their choice. There is some new, albeit small, competition in the search marketplace. As mentioned before I am an adviser to Andi search, a new way of searching the internet. It has a high level of data protection and is ad-free with no data tracking, so your searches are not spam based on ads that bid for your attention. Jeremy White is the founder of Andi search and he told me, 'If you're building a system like a GPT-based LLM, everything looks like a language problem' and not everything is a language problem.

Thoughtful data scientists have claimed to have found ways of AI self-learning and self-questioning, much like a human would do, asking new questions from the knowledge they have acquired. Titled 'Large Language Models Can Self-Improve', a group of researchers built an LLM that can come up with a set of questions, generate detailed answers to those questions, filter its own answers for the most high-quality output, and then fine-tune itself on the curated answers.

At the time of writing, there are claims of AI fact-checking and also evidence that there are a lot of 'facts' in AI that are not true. It's evolving and the only thing I can be sure about is this is likely to be the slowest rate of AI development we will ever see. We may end up subscribing to AI truth verification detecting apps.

The driverless car is a good analogy for the new type of decision-making that will be required in companies as we become enabled by DaaS. The driverless car needs to know much of the same high-level views required by directors and executives:

- Where am I, precisely?
- What is going on around me (other cars, pedestrians, roadworks, traffic lights, roundabouts, merging lanes, turning lanes, weather)?
- What will or might happen next (red light, green light, arrow light, random pedestrian on the road, car overtaking, car running a give way sign)?
- What should I do now (nothing, something)? What intervention is the best next move?

The AI powering the decisions of the car are, in theory, much less distracted than humans and are only getting better with the increasing amount of data being fed into them by the computers on new cars.

We need to be sure that any driverless cars are safe of course. We have due concerns about the driverless cars' safety and we should also have concerns about many bad human drivers.

The photo below shows what the computer systems see in a driverless car and how this compares to the human vision. What I find so fascinating is how the cognitive layers of the driverless cars are making billions of predictions, and so is the human driver. Will the bike rider suddenly move into my lane? How does this bike rider compare to others I have witnessed? What could be behind the trees to the right? The human driver can benchmark to what they individually know, whereas the machine can benchmark to a near-limitless number of precedents. A pothole ahead would be known by the driverless cars that follow; the human will notice it for the first time when they hit it.

Bias in decision-making

All decisions are made with bias. Each of us has our own 'reality' based on our lived experience. If you were bitten by a Cavalier King Charles as a child, it would likely make you look at all Cavaliers in a particularly biased way, and perhaps all dogs that look like that breed. It is a limited data set (of one) that frames the most powerful reference. Without a lot more data, such as knowing if King Charles Cavaliers bite more children than other dogs, and if that was true (and it is not), then individual bias is just that, individual bias, based on personal and highly emotional small data sets. The hard part in negating bias is opening up the data to verify if it's true, or if it is my pre-existing belief that is wrong and not based on anything beyond my sample of one.

Next time you are in a disagreement with someone, try this, and ask, 'What evidence can be brought to bear that would make you change your mind?' If the person says nothing can make them change their mind you now know you have entered an ideological debate devoid of facts.

Warren Buffett is purported to ask the following question in meetings quite often. 'What is it that you were once sure about that you've now changed your mind about?' In other words, what is it that you were wrong about before? So, the question to you and your colleagues, direct reports, your CEO/board is, 'What are we all wrong about? What is it that we are collectively all wrong about, and what myths do we have that need to be busted?'

Following the data requires a change of mindset, an openness and inquisitiveness along with wider organisational learning. For everyone the question needs to be, what data can be sourced that would make you pause and reflect on what you assume to be true?

In *The Premonition*, Michael Lewis talks about biases in the health industry with specific reference to the global pandemic. 'The differences between data bias, through algorithms and AI, and human bias is, ironically, the lot of human bias has no fingerprint as it is inside a head that can't be seen, understood or audited.'[74]

As Jonathan Grudin, a researcher at Microsoft, noted, 'The algorithms are not in control; people create and adjust them.' Humans can and do bias the output at multiple levels, from the data people choose to include to how the programmer chooses to build the algorithm. With data and AI, your organisation's use of data can and should be auditable and trackable, and that is a governance issue. If you code in a bad outcome it will ultimately land at the board's feet. What your data does or does not do is now a material board issue.

There are hundreds, if not thousands, of examples of bias using data from policing policies being skewed to specific ethnic minorities or socio-economic areas; the way job applications are handled,[75] credit card offers and rates[76] (even Apple's co-founder Steve Wozniak came face to face with bias), Amazon's hiring processes, and so on. Princeton University researchers found that European names were perceived as more pleasant than those of African Americans, and that the words woman and girl were more likely to be associated with the arts instead of science and math, which were most likely connected to males.[77]

There is a growing need to ensure the challenges of bias in AI and machine learning are mitigated and there are now specialist companies that interrogate your underlying data sets and models. These are designed to spot biases in algorithms by running synthetic data models before real deployment, if you don't have these capacities in-house. Accounts are audited, so the board has more comfort; it's now time to consider a data and algorithmic audit.

Separately, there is and will be more regulation and oversight by governments around AI and bias. The European Union has tasked a team of AI professionals to define a framework to help characterise AI risk and bias. The EU Artificial Intelligence Act (EU AIA) is intended to form a blueprint for human agency and oversight of AI, including guidelines for robustness, privacy, transparency, diversity, well-being and accountability.

---

74 *The Premonition: A Pandemic Story,* Michael Lewis, W W Norton, 2021.

75 https://thenextweb.com/news/study-shows-how-ai-exacerbates-recruitment-bias-against-women.

76 https://www.wired.com/story/the-apple-card-didnt-see-genderand-thats-the-problem/.

77 https://www.brookings.edu/research/algorithmic-bias-detection-and-mitigation-best-practices-and-policies-to-reduce-consumer-harms/.

The working group has also developed seven key principles for AI trust-worthiness that are worth summarising here so that you can incorporate these into discussions within your own organisation.

This is not an exhaustive list, but it's a good starting point:

1. Human agency and oversight
2. Technical robustness and safety
3. Privacy and data governance
4. Transparency
5. Diversity, non-discrimination and fairness
6. Societal and environmental well-being
7. Accountability[78]

In addition, there are actions companies can take across the whole organisation. This is not limited to the data and AI teams, it's a whole-of-company approach from the board and executive through to the front line including all business units, as well as in the assessment made of the platforms, models, consultants and data sets they contract and use:

1. Have a diverse team working on the models.
2. Understand your underlying data sets and models.
3. Be transparent and approachable.
4. Develop review processes to instil rigour in outcomes that do no harm.
5. Ensure security and privacy of customer data.
6. Engage external organisations such as the St James Ethics Centre and the Australian National Data Service in Australia, or similar highly respected organisations in other countries.

Decision-making with or without AI

Decision-making and human bias are all around us. In the book *Subliminal*, Leonard Mlodinow cites studies where people who had witnessed serious crimes, like bank robberies, were sent to a line-up, sometimes within 24 hours of the crime. Their failure rate to recognise the suspect has ranged between 30% and 50% even after strong visual contact. Many times, people actually picked police officers who had been put into the line-up. A human being's ability to recall information, even in a highly focused event that had 100% of their cognitive focus, is low. The video footage of an armed hold-up holds

---

78 https://towardsdatascience.com/seven-steps-to-help-you-reduce-bias-in-algorithms-in-light-of-the-eus-trustworthy-ai-blueprint-b348dc3cf2ae.

more reliable data, you could argue, than the recollection of the people who saw the crime.

When you ask a shopper why they buy your brand of washing powder, their cognitive processes are not necessarily fired up, and so the chances of getting a factual answer are low. Yet these shopper surveys are deemed to be powerful signals as we've witnessed. In Chapter 2 we covered Coca-Cola's change to its formula based on small focus groups, deciding the destiny of product launches or failures. In the world of AI: Game On, you can move from a sample size of N = 100 to N = all. That is not a small change in capacity to understand your customers. In 2011 there was a study of judges – highly educated and trained people – making vastly different decisions over very simple laws. The study examined judicial rulings by Israeli judges who presided over parole hearings in criminal cases. One of the co-authors of the peer-reviewed paper, Jonathan Levav, found that judges gave more lenient decisions at the start of the day and immediately after a scheduled break in court proceedings such as lunch. The research looked at more than 1,000 rulings made in 2009 by eight judges. They found that the likelihood of a favourable ruling peaked at the beginning of the day, steadily declining over time from a probability of about 65% to nearly zero, before spiking back up to about 65% after a break for a meal or snack.[79]

Levav went on to note that the exact reason for the shift from parole approval to a 'default' outcome of denial was not clear, but the paper speculated that breaks may replenish mental resources by providing 'rest, improving mood or by increasing glucose levels in the body'.

We're human after all, and that's the point.

Human beings are not designed for high-stakes, high-frequency decision-making. We are so quick to judge a machine's decision as flawed, simply because we can measure the inputs and observe the errors. It is not easy to observe human errors, as we tend to retrofit information back into why we made the decision. If the same judge can make a different decision based on their feelings due to the recency of their last meal, we have a problem with human decision-making that needs some reflection against those made by machines today, without even allowing for the machines of tomorrow.

---

79 https://www.theguardian.com/law/2011/apr/11/judges-lenient-break.

What questions should we be asking?

The questions we ask define us. When Einstein was 16 he tried to imagine he was chasing a beam of light to get a different perspective on what light is. It's a simple but great example of where human thought creates breakthrough innovation. The human mind will be a critical input into innovation for a long time to come. It is this expansive thinking and questioning, what would it be like to be on a beam of light moving at light speed, that opened up Einstein's insights. This sort of thinking may well be the last frontier for AI to challenge humankind on. This creative thinking is where humans can spend more time, once smaller decisions are industrialised into ethically safe AI and data systems.

Two good questions to ask of your data that hold significant value if you can answer them well are: 'Which customer will defect from our product and service and why?' These are key questions linked to the future enterprise valuation of the business.

Defection is predictable in most cases, yet if you ask questions like these in most boardrooms you may well be met with one of the following responses: that is an operational matter not concerning the board, or we don't have the data to accurately know, but our gut feel is XYZ. Both answers are dangerous and may well be key signs your organisation is heading the way of the taxi industry. The silent voice of the real defecting customer is gold, as that voice – or more likely data flow – is showing your product or services has flaws that relate to their existing or future needs.

'What is the unmet need of our future customers?' This is where strategy can be created. (This prediction could be a book in itself, and I look at this in the last chapter.)

The value of any business is determined by the future cash flow of the customers. The future unmet need of your customer is the future value of the business, if you can find it and solve it. Motorola and Yahoo failed to find their customers' future needs and others did – Apple and Google – and the change continues with new entrants and new business models.

Finding 'the answer' in business

We live in a world where if the answer exists, you can find it in one click, so most answers to any basic question are no longer hard to find. The new challenge facing boards and executives is what questions can add to the collective value. Questions such as:

- What new data could be found in our business that would answer and frame new questions?

- What data do we have that may hold value today and tomorrow?

- What ethically sourced external data could be obtained that allows us to know what our customers do when they are not interacting with our product or service?

- How can we get to the future needs of our customers before our competitors?

- What would real AI capability add to our products and services?

In a world of data and AI, new questions can be asked of existing and new data. The answers can be delivered at the speed of light, actioned across all customers, and measured for all customers, then reprogramed from all insights, a perpetual and ever-improving OODA loop of action, insight, with more actions, more data, more insights.

A learning machine that serves customers is the engine room of the AI: Game On companies of tomorrow

CHAPTER TAKEAWAYS

1. AI and data-driven decision-making are transforming industries and offering new possibilities for innovation. Yet far too many are still just talking about AI. Having the first, material use case is vital as a defensive moat, and builds momentum that can lead to a new business model.

2. The OODA loop and differentiation between Type 1 and Type 2 decisions can help companies avoid slowing down innovation.

3. Governance frameworks are crucial for ensuring AI and data operations are trustworthy and reliable and must always protect and advance human dignity.

4. Biases can affect decisions in various areas, and synthetic data models and testing can help identify them.

5. Customer signals can get lost, blocked or distorted between the front line and the boardroom, so it is vital to make sure you are getting an objective set of signals from your customers, including those who defect.

Chapter 7

DATA AT THE HEART OF THE WHOLE COMPANY

'Find products for your customers not customers for your product.'
– Seth Godin

As chair of the NRMA, I have had the privilege to meet the Australian CEOs of many of the largest car companies in the world. The automotive industry is a giant and is the second largest expenditure most people make in their lifetime. Yet outside Tesla, real data use and deep embedded customer interaction systems are undeveloped. Most traditional car manufacturers are disconnected from the end customer via poor data strategy and dealership models that outsource the customer relationship.

I recently asked the CEO of one of the large Japanese automotive firms how they predicted demand by car type and location. He said, 'We don't really, the factory largely allocates us the make, model, features and colours. In reality, a country like Australia is at the end of the output to the factory in Japan.' I was stunned, naively thinking it would be a meticulous data-driven process, using analytics to predict demand by location to build up to that total forecast. What happens is basically a factory 10,000 kilometres away pumps out cars with no real data on the true localised demand of the market. Good executives do their best to allocate the cars to the dealers, from spreadsheets and/or simple demand forecasting tools and dealer requests. It is a long way from the way Amazon uses a patented IP to predict which of their hundreds of millions of customers will buy each of their millions of products.

In today's data-rich world there is a way to predict demand by household for new cars on a de-identified probability basis. This can be done without personal information (PI). The location of the existing fleet of all cars is known, databases exist of registration, location of dealerships, and the churn of the ownership are all knowable and this can be fed into a prediction for purchase.

A propensity score to buy a new car could be created for every home. The value of the home is one proxy for the type of car model. Owners of $20 million harbourfront homes may be driving a 15-year-old Mazda, but it is mathematically more likely that this type of homeowner will own a prestige car. I spoke with a brilliant data scientist I know who said he could build a model that basically asks this question: How likely is this pod of 10 residential homes to buy, say a Toyota Corolla, this year using every available data set on a de-identified basis? Repeat for all homes and you've created a forecast by location for that brand of car. You could run this model against real sales data and improve its performance continually. This makes allocation from the factory better, and importantly, allocation by location in the country much more relevant. This is how a retail giant like Walmart would view this challenge to allocate each item they stock, using data, to predict demand by location, time, season and time of day. If it's worth doing for cat food, it would be worth doing for cars with a much higher value. If the organisation's culture is not one of data-driven innovation it will end up being challenged by a new entrant that will be data-driven.

Highly predictive models change the cost curve for the industry and allow customers to find what they want at the right time and right place. This would be a revolution for car companies and their dealers that currently struggle with having too many of the wrong cars that need to be discounted or long wait lists for the cars in high demand. Both these issues cost the industry billions around the globe. A customer-centric data-driven approach could help the industry to better supply cars. A by-product of such a predictive model could be a recommendation engine for customers showing them the best time to trade in and what other buyers like them purchased. The consumer should have tools to help them do this sort of work and the car companies are well placed to service this need. Car retailing is changing, Tesla has started this trend and it's going to become a harder industry for data laggards.

We are at the point of a new evolutionary model of business, one in which the 'data vertebrate' has evolved to dominate the data invertebrate. Capturing signals from the real source of truth, the customer, and aligning the organisation to interpret and respond to these signals is what the predictive organisation do. Capturing data is one thing; creating an organisation that responds effectively is much harder.

At the time of writing, Tesla is opening up some of its charging stations to owners of non-Tesla vehicles. The charging stations can only be accessed via the Tesla app, so the benefit for the customer is more available charging stations. The benefit for Tesla is a one-to-one connection with the owners of EVs outside of the Tesla universe. Other car companies are largely still disconnected from the end user, whereas Tesla has created a value exchange that will allow them into their competitors' minds, phones and wallets.

In his book *Post Corona*, Scott Galloway makes the point that: 'There are two fundamental business models; one, a company can sell stuff for more than the cost of making it. Apple takes $400 worth of circuits and glass and imbues it with a promise of status and sex appeal through brilliant advertising, and charges me $1,200 for an iPhone. Two, a company can give stuff away, or sell it below cost and charge other companies for access to its consumers' behavioural data.'[80]

His points are valid and the trade each of us undertakes with a company for allowing the use of our data is complex. In the simplest terms, you need to make sure the customer receives real value and that you don't harm them in the process.

Galloway sees the world dividing into those companies that strive to protect customer data and make a virtue out of their data strategy, and those where it's 'data game on', using all customer data available to extract maximum value. The critical factor for companies to consider is a combination of the data use case, transparency with the customer, and what's in it for the customer.

> **'Every company these days is basically in the data business and they're going to need AI to civilise and digest big data and make sense out of it – big data without AI is a big headache.'**
> – Kevin Kelly

More companies are embedding artificial intelligence in their products, services, processes and decision-making. AI has now shifted from a 'nice-to-have' to a 'must-have' technology, yet BCG noted in a recent article that 'while many companies have invested in AI only 11% have realised significant value from these investments.'[81]

---

80 Scott Galloway, *Post Corona: From Crisis to Opportunity*, Bantam Press.

81 https://venturebeat.com/2021/09/29/ignoring-data-comes-at-a-price-report-finds/.

For those entering the field of data analytics today it is unimaginable what it was like when I entered it many years ago. In those days, if I talked to a CEO or board members about using data and AI to help drive change, strategy, deliver better customer experiences, optimisation, any use at all, they would tend to look at me as though they thought I was referring to their IT department (with some notable exceptions) and politely suggest that I talk to the 'tech guys' down the hall as 'they were the ones who worried about data.'

In the company I was working with at the time (Quantium) we developed the view that if the C-suite sent you to the tech team, it was a real indicator that the business was in trouble. The C-suite were hoping they could delegate this key strategic initiative to the tech team. Today AI adoption, data use, customer-centricity and governance are at the forefront of many businesses and key agenda items for boards.

Data and AI strategy are now the business strategy

Data strategy now feeds into the AI playbook.
It is evolving so fast with such profound consequences
that it must be the central business strategy.

Businesses are now in a place where they do not need a data strategy within their business. They need a business strategy, driven by data, enabled with AI that guides all strategic initiatives, digital or not. As McKinsey noted 'The CX programs of the future will be holistic, predictive, precise and clearly tied to business outcomes.'

Over the last 15 years I have presented to hundreds of board directors on what the boardroom dashboard will look like in the next few years. The key metrics most businesses run by and report to have changed little over the last 20 years, even though their enterprise has changed dramatically. The bulk of board reports still don't focus on the future intentions and behaviours of their customers – that is, harnessing the predictive insights of data. Next time you are preparing a board report or you receive one ask, 'Where is the customer in all this?' and see what response you get.

When data is this accessible and dynamic, we can envisage different types of board and executive discussions. What are the customers doing with our product? Where do they go when they leave us? What did we do that led to growth or contraction? You can now see and hear actual customer con-versations with your field force with opt-in approval. These can be made into text summaries, and with sentiment analysis. There are some progressive companies that, on occasion, let their front-line team request to record conversations with the customer, with the explicit reason that they believe the CEO should hear it. No filter can be very powerful.

John Chambers, who was chairman of Cisco when I spoke with him a few years ago, understood the challenges of changing to a data-led organisation:

> The hard part is how do you change your organisation structure? How do you change your culture to be able to think in terms of outcomes for your customers? Today, you're talking about digitisation being an integral part of the fabric of a company's business strategy or the way it interfaces its supply chain with its customers. Not enabled by technology – technology will become the company.[82]

The chart below is a real case study where a retailer used customer behavioural data to frame up an acquisition target. It was not an investment bank's pitch; it was an acquisition driven by customers' needs. The target was selected from de-identified bank data that showed purchase behaviours.

Finding merger targets is still largely an analogue old-school business with people in suits talking about good ideas over lunch and coffee in the main. Algorithmic merger targets are coming that look at the logic in a data-driven way around customer fit and other parameters.

DATA DRIVEN **M&A**

How data driven M&A activity would occur

---

82 https://www.mckinsey.com/industries/technology-media-and-telecommunications/our-insights/ciscos-john-chambers-on-the-digital-era.

Data use in every part of your business

Marketing managers' roles are unrecognisable from what they were at the dawn of the data revolution back in the late 1980s and '90s. Marketing teams from decades ago spent time at long lunches with ponytailed creatives talking about TV ads and magazine campaigns (I should know – I was part of this and it was fun!). Today, leading marketing teams and agencies are data-driven. If you want to understand marketing in a data-driven world read Sinan Arai's book *The Hype Machine* where he explores the science behind the new technologies and modes of communication underpinned by data – personalised mass persuasion via integrated digital marketing. I know one highly successful insurance company where the marketing director is an actuary, studying response rates, deploying algorithms, buying audiences in a bidding machine, more like a Bloomberg terminal for stocks at the speed of light. Many are using third-party data houses and collaborations to harness the power of massive, interconnected data sets.

Nineteenth-century Philadelphia retailer John Wanamaker supposedly said, 'Half the money I spend on advertising is wasted; the trouble is I don't know which half.' This was how marketing was seen. Today, with real-time attribution, wastage can and should be much less and targeting can be very sophisticated, provided you are not being sucked in by measuring and paying for the wrong outcomes. (See Arai's commentary in the footnote link about the gross overselling of the effectiveness of digital marketing, by a factor of three and sometimes by a factor of 10.[83])

You can easily buy an audience for people who like orange juice for breakfast, aged 45–49 and live in an apartment within 200 metres from your shop. But try to find out who in your team is overworked, and will resign next week. Yet the data to predict this is available, sitting in a server within HR departments not able to see the information until the resignation hits their desk.

HR is in for large-scale change as AI, scaled data and predictive capabilities are applied to this most 'human' of functions – managing people. I'm excited about this area and have invested in some early-stage companies that have different offerings for enterprises to use data allowing their teams to enjoy their work more, perform at a higher level, and feel more connected and supported.

The CEO of one of the many new companies in this space recently said to me, 'We are excited about what can be done with AI and analytics in HR. When you look at the other departments like procurement, marketing, new product development, we are seeing AI and large-scale predictive analytics being

---

83 *The Hype Machine*, ibid pages 145-155.

applied fast, yet the HR department is still using white boards and emails in many cases.'

The need to better align and connect with employees has been exacerbated by Covid-19 and what is known as 'the great resignation'. After being forced to work from home during the height of Covid and subsequent shorter lockdowns, many employees are now demanding the flexibility to build in a mixture of work from home and in the office. One AI-driven tool I have seen compares hybrid working days' metadata with days of flows where all the staff are on-site. They found some interesting insights right off the bat. Small short-term projects can be done with WFH very well. Long-term, complex collaborative projects were very unproductive in the WFH world. This is metadata from emails, slack channels and delivery of outputs. We know that for many companies if you don't offer this flexibility, employees are leaving. Your most talented staff will be the ones who will get the most offers.

The real issues around data, AI and human management are how to design systems to make them fair, to avoid unintended biases, and to ensure they don't become a management surveillance mechanism. That will be a one-way ticket to mass resignations.

HR supported by AI will soon be capable of asking and answering a wide range of more nuanced questions. For example:

- How can we measure the candidate's capacity to learn and thrive here?
- What emotional fitness/intelligence (EQ) is key to being a leader in our organisation?
- Which candidate will be the best hire?
- Which candidate could be the CEO in 10–15 years' time?
- Which staff members need support?
- Which staff members are at risk of overwork/burnout?
- Which manager helps staff in ways that make them happier about their work?
- How can we capture data about our high performers so we can predict who could create more of them?
- What behaviours in the team indicate the best team leader?
- What cultural risks can be mitigated with the use of AI data in the HR function?

When these sorts of questions are backed into a recruitment algorithm that can scan LinkedIn, looking for talent that will work for the organisation, the theory is it can create teams that are happy and high-performing. All these sorts of questions exist in the data that organisations already collect; it's likely, however, that the information is spread across various divisions, with specific individuals and not analytics-ready.

Remember street directories? For those of you who don't, there were books with maps of how to move around the city. Every car had one. It was a great business. Nowadays it's predictive analytics that uses real-time location and the baseline of the old maps that means drivers get real-time recommendations of which streets to use because of a traffic incident. Similarly, HR will move to a world of predictive analytics and the maps most HR teams use today will look like your old street directory in the glovebox. These are areas where data and AI are coming fast, and where HR teams will see much more change. An ethically driven approach using the data Hippocratic oath or something similar will be necessary.

Recruitment is being augmented with AI. Recently it was reported that Afterpay, Qantas, Spark NZ, Iceland Foods, Woodies (USA), among other companies, are using a bot called Phai to undertake the first interview of candidates. The Phai bot is a smart interviewer. It claims it can discover a person's personality traits from their written answers to questions. The company behind this is PredictiveHire. They have adapted Google's Bidirectional Encoder Representations from Transformers (BERT) — a natural language pre-training algorithm — using 1.3 million candidates, which has enabled PredictiveHire to accumulate a proprietary data set of 550 million words.[84] There are real ethical challenges coming in this use case and some new laws are already in place in the EU regarding hiring processes with AI.

While the focus of AI and data has been on marketing, the whole organisation is on its way to AI: Game On from better use and deployment of data and AI, including procurement, logistics, operations, capex, finance and more. The CEO of a Fortune top 30 Australian listed company shared with me recently his view that 'there is no area of this business where a data-driven approach could not lead to a significant commercial impact'. He cited a $30 million EBIT impact as being available pretty much in every process in the business from logistics, M&A, finance, ESG, procurement and HR to new product design and even health and safety.

---

84   Afterpay, Woolworths use bot for interviews, Yolanda Redrup, *AFR*, 8 March 2022.

AI: Game On requires a culture change first

Can you change the culture of a company to one that has a thirst for data, as opposed to building a data-driven company? Absolutely. Just look at the change that occurred at Microsoft. Satya Nadella radically re-engineered how Microsoft operates both with its customers and other stakeholders. Microsoft's market capitalisation has more than tripled since they adopted this approach. Linked to this is Nadella's approach to learning.

Presentation by Satya Nadella

We are in the business of meeting the unmet, unarticulated needs of customers. That means you need a system that finds the unmet and unarticulated needs. No survey can find the unarticulated clue of the customer. When I joined Microsoft's culture at the time was hard edged, quantitative, metric driven. To find the unmet unarticulated needs of the customer we had to change our culture and therefore the metrics we were using so that we could harness the signals of the customer in real time.

Harness the signals of the customer in real time

Alfred Chuang, the founder and CEO of BEA Systems (sold to Oracle for $8.6 billion) and founder of Race Capital, is one of the pioneers of predictive transaction processing. Chuang comments that 'for businesses to remain relevant and competitive they need to be able to predict customer behaviours and preferences and need to rely on predictive transactions to automate most of their business interactions.'[85]

In other words, it required the move from data and AI-enhancing decisions to predicting outcomes and next best action. He cites TikTok as one of the world leaders in this. Its algorithm 'sees' what you watch and gives you more of it, and learns from every clip you watch.[86] I'm not a fan of the addictive nature of some of these tools designed to take our attention. However, their capacity to find the customers' interest and attention is both scary and incredible. It's the use case that matters. If the attention was paid to how one might create a better eating regime, that is very different to how to sit on the couch and watch cats dancing.

Alphabet has launched a company that uses AI for drug discovery built on research carried out by AI Lab. As part of this, Google acquired DeepMind in 2014 and launched Isomorphic Labs with the mission to 'reimagine the entire

---

85 https://medium.com/@alfred_chuang/the-future-of-computing-is-here-predictive-transaction-processing-3230e733d3ab.

86 Ibid.

drug discovery process from the ground up. Not only does the AI analyse data but it also builds powerful predictive and generative models of complex biological phenomena that have led to breakthroughs in protein folding. One model has accurately predicted how the structure of proteins will fold in a matter of days, something that has eluded scientists for decades.'[87]

Xavier Shay, chief executive of neobank Up (acquired by Bendigo Bank through its acquisition of Ferocia in January 2022), comments that 'people are now seeing you can get a tech experience that's up there with Netflix and Uber [in banking]'. If you're not afraid of Square, then you're not paying attention. It's not just Square, it's pretty much all of the big tech players in Apple, Google, Amazon, and I think they all have the same game plan.'[88] In April 2023 Apple launched its banking business. They will have data advantages, brand trust and technology capabilities that the traditional banks will not have. Watch this space.

JPMorgan Chase recently announced that it would spend $16.7 billion on developing new technology to avoid being disrupted by the neobanks.

Data and AI are vital to you, now

Imagine a scenario where, say, a venue becomes much more than that. For example, what if a customer's iris is scanned as part of their entry. That scan could be used to identify certain medical issues, ones that could be success-fully treated because of this early awareness. The customer may find this helpful, so long as they know what the machine is doing on their behalf and the same data is not sent to anyone else.

In this imaginary case and with the use of data that is visible, actionable, and transparent to the customer, the value impact of the data use can allow the venue operator to tap a value pool well outside of their traditional revenue lines. There is enormous value in the 'product of the product'. The product is a venue and whatever happens in the venue, but that entry scan and the movement of high numbers of people can create a myriad of other large-scale impacts.

Increasingly, we will see data-driven balance sheets. Historically, the basis for every company's share price and valuation has been a combination of discounted cash flows, internal rates of returns, revenue growth, P/E ratio, EBITDA margin, EV/EBITDA ratio and so on. These are all based on models

87 BCG, AI ready to ride the wave, https://www.bcg.com/en-au/featured-insights/executive-perspectives.

88 Big Tech threat stares down at Aussie banks, Ayesha de Krester, AFR, 19 January 2022, page 13.

about future revenues and costs. Where is the future revenue coming from? Customers! If you really understand customers and what they want, you can much better predict revenues and therefore valuations. Put it this way, if you are in a company that has a forecast, budget and business plan, you are predicting customers' spending. Yet for all the care that goes into this, too many companies fail to look at the drivers of customer behaviours that make up the forward cash flow. This is starting to alter, and it will make customer predictions count in the boardroom in new ways.

Imagine if your business had a more accurate and predictive model of future customer behaviours

There's a model already being used by some of the world's leading data/AI-driven companies, as well as by shareholders, investors, fund managers and financial institutions. It is called customer-based company valuation (CBCV) and it's based on deep data about customers. A recent article in *Harvard Business Review (HBR)* cites the IPO of Revolve in the USA, an e-commerce platform that caters to millennial and Generation Z consumers by curating luxury apparel, footwear and accessory items. The IPO was priced at $1.2 billion and exploded on its first day by 89%, giving it a valuation of 4.5 times its previous 12-month revenue, 'more like a tech company than a clothing company'.[89] Why did this happen? To quote *HBR*, 'Revolve's premium valuation was not a fluke. It stemmed from the firm's strong underlying fundamentals, which were not fully appreciated by the underwriters who set the IPO price. This strength was less about top-line revenue growth and more about strong customer-unit economics: Simply put, Revolve not only acquired its customers profitably but retained them for many years, and that meant its longer-term profit potential was larger than its revenue growth to date had implied.'

Using data to price assets is emerging – another governance issue in waiting. Directors who are signing off on valuations of assets will need to understand what data was used and what impact that has on valuations.

If you haven't come across CBCV perhaps you have heard of C3 (customer cohort charts). These charts track revenue by acquisition cohort over time and show how total customer spending changes as each cohort ages. Companies such as Slack, Lyft, Dropbox, Farfetch, Backblaze and ZooPlus integrate C3 charts into their quarterly, half-yearly and yearly reporting packs to better enable shareholders and investors to evaluate their future business.[90] [91]

---

89 https://store.hbr.org/product/how-to-value-a-company-by-analyzing-its-customers/s20012?sku=S20012-PDF-ENG.

90 https://thetaclv.com/resource/c3/.

91 https://www.steveripplinger.com/posts/backblaze-customer-analytics.

Data and AI bring a higher degree of precision, accountability and diagnostics to value customers in the new loyalty economy. Netflix, Verizon, Spotify, Activision, Blizzard (acquired by Microsoft for US$68 billion in October 2023),[92] Zipcar and Peloton are just some of the leaders in the subscription loyalty economy. We are seeing the subscription of everything evolving, from cars to travel and retail just to name a few.

As an executive, director or leader in your business, the questions you may have are: Where does the ethical use of AI bring the most competitive advantage? Is it in products, services, processes, decision-making, new business models – or all of the above?

AI has already migrated from simply finding relationships and predicting trends. It is now capable of spotting (predicting) future shifts by analysing preferences and sentiments using vast quantities of your own data – as well as text, voice, images, digital, newsfeeds, social media and global data-banks.

When talking to John Chambers while he was global chairman of Cisco, his view, which I share, is that boardroom dashboards should be focused on future events, based on customers' needs with less time looking in the rear-view, and more time predicting what is next best action for the organisation. The static historic numbers from last month will soon change to immersive virtual walkthroughs of the real-time data – a control room where streaming data is alive and where you can hear the calls of the customers, feel the strength of the demand and the nuance of the changes in the market.

The boardroom of the future is set to become less of a slideshow and more immersive flight deck simulator, with real-time customer-centric information.

Leveraging AI as a business transformation opportunity

BCG presents one model for large-scale adoption of data and AI. It is a methodology based on extensive research across 3,000 respondents from 29 industries and 112 countries. Their model focuses on two core themes: embedding AI into your business and preparing your operating model for AI across three core building blocks: data, processing and action.

BCG's model provides a four-step approach to unlocking the financial benefits of AI, which involves reimagining the way your company works with data and an ability to move from pilot to scaling. The model looks like this:

---

92   https://www.afr.com/companies/games-and-wagering/microsoft-s-bet-on-activision-sets-off-content-wars-in-gaming-20220120-p59pxf.

1. Discover AI – Launch pilots in key areas.

2. Build AI – Embed in overall strategy; reimagine use of data; invest in data capability building, technology, and algorithms and in developing technical AI skills.

3. Scale AI – Broader use cases and solutions. Embed AI into processes and solutions on both production and consumption sides.

4. Organisational learning with AI – Create opportunities for mutual learning between humans and AI.[93]

External data and data ecosystems

Leading AI companies are harnessing the insights of their own data as well as that of third-party data companies sourced within ethical and data use guard rails. If your first-party data is not available and usable, you may need other data sets to help get to the unmet needs of your customers. Noting that first-party data should be your first port of call since it's yours and it will typically be unique to your organisation. So, if you can access first-party data, you should regard it as an asset, so long as it has been collected ethically. An increasing number of companies are building businesses on the Internet of Data and Computing (IoDC), commonly referred to as collaborative data ecosystems. Woolworths Australia has done this through their partnership with Quantium, and now CBA and Telstra have also created ventures with Quantium. These allow their own business needs to be built at scale, and also for their partners. Amazon Web Services (AWS) offers such an ecosystem as does Teradata, Databricks, Alibaba and BaseBit to name just a few, alongside significant data ecosystems in the health, education and government services areas.

The benefits of collaborative data ecosystems are significant. A Capgemini report noted that 'organisations that use more than seven data sources have nearly 14 times the fixed-asset turnover and two times the market capitalisation compared to organisations who do not use any external data for decision making'.[94]

---

93 https://www.bcg.com/en-au/featured-insights/executive-perspectives.

94 https://www.capgemini.com/au-en/service/perform-ai/collaborative-data-ecosystems/.

You are what you measure

Data without context and clarity is almost as useless as not looking at the data at all. On a recent podcast (Pivot),[95] Professor Scott Galloway discussed some recent analyses of the top American universities that showed that the traditional sandstone universities of Harvard, Yale, Princeton and others are always at the top of the list of high-performing graduates. He went on to say that, of course, these universities would be top performers because they rejected, in some cases, over 96% of all applicants. If your input cohort of students are from the brightest 4% of the total pool you are very likely to have graduates with the top scores. It's then a decision about what to measure. N = only smart kids v N = all. If you changed how universities were being rewarded and funded to say, their ability to uplift students' capabilities, they would not only take the top 4%.

This type of discussion takes us straight to questions about the use and impact of data: What problem is trying to be solved, and what are the data sets that help you solve that problem?

As data becomes more transparent and accessible it is not hard to imagine new business use cases. Imagine a new type of insurance business where you go to your cohort of LinkedIn friends who might all be of similar economic status to yourself. You know these people are very unlikely to commit fraud, and are largely low-claim risks. This model could be developed to a point where the cohort actually becomes the underwriter of insurance. As we move into a world of AI-enabled personalised bots, vast numbers of new ways of using AI and data will be developed.

'It is not the strongest of the species that survives,
nor the most intelligent; it is the one most adaptable to change.'
— Charles Darwin

In the next chapter we look at the data journey, how to start the journey, the culture you need to build, the options available to you depending on where your organisation is currently, and more of what's at the forefront of data and AI right now.

95 https://podcasts.apple.com/au/podcast/pivot/id1073226719.

CHAPTER TAKEAWAYS

1. The new evolutionary model of business is data-driven and requires companies to adopt AI to interpret and respond to customer signals.

2. Companies don't need a data strategy as their entire business strategy must be driven by data and enabled with AI to guide all strategic initiatives.

3. Predicting customer behaviour is critical to remaining competitive and this needs to be well understood in the boardroom.

4. The boardroom of the future should focus more on future events based on customers' needs and use tools such as immersive virtual walkthroughs of real-time data.

5. Data when seen as an ecosystem creates more value. Organisations that use more than seven data sources have nearly 14 times the fixed-asset turnover and two times the market capitalisation compared to peers who do not use external data for decision-making.

Chapter 8

THE DATA AI JOURNEY

It has been 40-plus years since John Naisbitt, author of *Megatrends*, wrote, 'We are drowning in information but starved for knowledge.' A lot has changed, and the world has polarised into organisations that are strong on using information, data and now AI and the others who are still trying to find their way in this new operating environment.

> 'The heaviest weight in the gym is the front door.'
> — American boxer Ed Latimore

Data and AI are your business's heartbeat and circulatory system

In 2016 Kevin Kelly wrote *The Inevitable: Understanding the 12 Technological Forces That Will Shape Our World*. The underpinning concept of his book is that at the centre of every significant change in our lives today is a technology of some sort.

> 'Technology is humanity's accelerant. Because of technology everything we make is always in the process of becoming. Every kind of thing is becoming something else ... Nothing is finished. Nothing is done. Constant flux means more than simply things will be different. It means processes are now more important than products.' [96]

---

96 *The Inevitable*, Kevin Kelly, 2016, page 6.

Generative AI tools are a great example of this point, as processes and capabilities are now able to create the next iteration. Like the notion of atomic fusion and its perpetual energy promise, generative AI is perpetual programming improvement.

Data has been said to be the 'new oil'. I disagree with this analogy. Oil as it relates to petrol is a 'use once' product: refine, use, done, with its externality of carbon emissions. Data is much more sustainable with its life cycle being more like refine, use, reuse, blend, augment with other data, new use cases remodel, refine, and on it goes. Medical researchers are using DNA collected decades ago to great effect in drug discovery. Data can be valuable over time and use.

A report by McKinsey Global Institute estimated 'liquid' information that is machine-readable, accessible to a broad audience at little or no cost, and capable of being shared and distributed could generate an additional $3 trillion in economic activity, enabling applications as diverse as self-driving cars, personalised healthcare and traceable food supply chains.[97]

The increased feasibility of sharing data is being accelerated by the proliferation of data sources through the Internet of Things (IoT). In addition, there are new techniques, protocols and standards for pooling, sharing and exchanging data. Knowledge through the exchange of data is part of a new European Union data strategy. It is designed to create 'a single market for data' to empower people, business and organisations to make better decisions based on insights from non-personal data in order to compete with the current tech giants.[98] In Australia open banking was introduced after the Australian Government passed legislation, called Consumer Data Rights. It empowers the customer to share their banking data with any accredited organisation.

However, capturing and adding all this data to existing (legacy) and new business systems is also creating confusion about how to find it, use it, manage it, and legally, securely and efficiently share it. Where did a certain data set come from? Who owns what? Have we legally sourced it? Have we ethically dealt with it, and have we protected it? Who's allowed to see certain things? Where does it reside? Can it be shared? Can it be sold? Can people see how it was used? And, most importantly, what is its purpose? This last question may seem obvious but in many companies I've worked with the answer differs depending on who you are talking to, at what level, and in which division (silo) they belong.

---

97 https://www.ced.org/blog/entry/big-datas-economic-impact https://www.mckinsey.com/~/media/mckinsey/industries/public%20and%20social%20sector/our%20insights/how%20government%20can%20promote%20open%20data/how_govt_can_promote_open_data_and_help_unleash_over_$3_trillion_in_economic_value.pdf.

98 https://digital-strategy.ec.europa.eu/en/policies/open-data.

As data applications grow and become more ubiquitous, consumers, owners and stewards of data are finding that they don't have a playbook to follow. Consumers want to connect to data they trust so they can make the best possible decisions. Owners of the data need tools to share their data safely with those who need it. Risk registers need to adapt to the reality of our times with cybercrime and ransomware widespread.

The board's dilemma comes down to one thing: managing risk in a world of VUCA — volatility, uncertainty, complexity and ambiguity. Data misuse and cyber hacks are already on the risk register of most boards. The lack of data use and not being competitive with data and AI need to be added to the risk register too.

How can you protect the crown jewels of data in the organisation and use it optimally at the same time? Lock it up and you get no customer benefit, open it up and you get hacked. It is wise to start with an audit of what you have data-wise, why you have it, how you obtained it, what has and could it be used for.

This is where you may need outside help. If data is not your core competency, get help from experts. Companies that do this work 24/7 are a long way along the experience curve.

Data is the product

Increasingly the data is the product. Fitbits are a relatively simple device; it's the data dashboards for the user that hold much of the value for them, while the company that owns Fitbit (Google from 2021) acquires yet more data for its businesses and can continuously improve a range of its products and offerings. Fitbit has over 120 million devices used by millions of users. Waze (also bought by Google in 2013) is yet another example where the data of the customer, while driving, is an input into the product. By using Waze I give the company data about where I am driving, how the traffic flow is working, or other information, while receiving valuable information from them about my ETA, traffic con-gestion, hazards and more. It suggests changes to my drive based on information from other users so the system gets smarter with more users.

The 'give to get' model of data is upon us across many areas of our life. Just consider the apps you use on a daily basis. Many are 'free' because the value exchange is your information/data, such as those from Facebook, Twitter, Booking.com, Findr, Strava, Under Armour's MapMyRun, Everyday Rewards, FlyBuys and more.

The synergy of data and AI and humans

Much of the discussion around data, AI and machine learning has focused on the impact on the workforce or, more specifically, the displacement of humans in the workplace and fear around lost occupations and jobs. This makes great headlines, but the realities are harder to predict. I am not saying there won't be major changes in the jobs, occupations and professions of the future but technology has always resulted in structural adjustment that requires shifting skills and workplace changes. Professor Richard Baldwin at the Geneva Graduate Institute in Switzerland, recently said about Artificial Intelligence. "AI won't take your job, It is somebody using AI that will take your job."

Perhaps for the next 20 years AI and machine learning seem less likely to substitute human intelligence, and rather they will augment it. There is ultimately a handoff from the machine to the human. That handoff is the Spotify playlist, the new antibiotic, the plane landing, the parcel delivered by the drone. So, the value comes from the augmentation back to humans. I like to use the term augmented for AI rather than artificial for just this reason. The data AI quest to create a better customer experience and complete the journey to a genuine understanding of the customer remains the key first-level priority of using data.

'Hiding within those mounds of data is the knowledge that could change the life of a patient or change the world.' – Atul Butte

At a pro bono workshop with Australia's leading minds on pancreatic cancer, facilitated by Dr Norman Swan, I witnessed how data and analytics can help change the trajectory of medicine. Many of our leading experts on pancreatic cancer were in the room talking about how this most brutal of cancers is both hard to detect early and how and why it has one of the lowest survival rates.

Greg Schneider, co-founder of Quantium, drew three columns on the white board. He said if in column 1 you had the DNA sequencing data of people who had and have had pancreatic cancer, then column 2 had all the medical interventions that had happened to this group of people in their life, and in column 3 you had all lifestyle factors of this group, and you linked the columns in a de-identified privacy-compliant way you would see new ways of understanding the disease immediately. Of course the people involved will need to approve their data for this use. It would show, for example, whether the use of antibiotics in childhood has any impact, positive or negative, on pancreatic cancer. Do high quantities of processed foods add any risk?

What DNA characteristics make individuals more vulnerable? Correlations and possible causation will be revealed in the data.

Greg knows nothing about medicine or pancreatic cancer, but a lot about how to use data. There was a gulp in the room as these medical minds could see how the data, used at scale and for the benefit of the patient, was a massive accelerant to the path forward for discovery of treatments and hopefully prevention.

As large-scale genetic information becomes securely available for medical science the acceleration of a more personalised medicine is set to advance faster.

The UK Biobank has an ambitious plan to sequence all life on earth. It's a large-scale ambitious project. Genomic sequencing has enabled improvements in drug discovery and increasingly medical breakthroughs are looking more like a data and maths challenge. Moderna vaccines for Covid were created quickly by using the genetic sequences of the virus and the virus itself was never on site. It was, according to Francis deSouza, CEO of Illumina, 'seen as a software problem'.

Medicine, like most aspects of life, will be more personalised in an AI data enabled future.

Your new segmentation strategy is a segment of one

Many organisations use data inputs for customer segmentation or understanding customers' preferences. When done at a basic level, and without human oversight, you can have some bizarre outcomes. As an example, let's take King Charles and Ozzy Osbourne, which was shared with me by Tony Davis, one of the founders of Quantium.

They were born in the same year, 1948. Both are in the high-wealth bracket, and spend a lot of time in the same location, London. They both like international travel, dogs, sports cars, fine wines, have children and have married and remarried. One might think they perhaps have different tastes in music but who knows? From a basic raw data perspective, they share a remarkable similarity. For some analytic engines that are based on simple metrics of age, gender, location and family status, they will appear as very similar, almost twins, in terms of how the simple algorithm sees them. Some companies whose segmentations are based on simple metrics, not related to real behaviours, would be sending the King of England and the king of heavy metal the same advertisements and the same product suggestions, no doubt annoying both of them. Neither would find such a scenario even remotely a good customer experience.

Any segmentation that is not a segment of one and full personalisation is set up to fail. Personalisation is now table stakes in consumer expectations. McKinsey agrees. They found 71% of consumers expect companies to deliver personalised interactions. And 76% get frustrated when this doesn't happen. The future of business, medicine and most industries will be personalised, driven by data. Data is the heartbeat of personalisation. You cannot personalise your offering if you don't really know the customer.

In the book *The Everything Store*, Brad Stone talks about how Jeff Bezos went to his board two decades ago to pitch the need for personalisation of all Amazon touchpoints that required hundreds of data scientists. When asked by his board, 'Why do you need all these data scientists?', he responded with words to the effect of: 'If we don't personalise everything somebody else will, and then we will be cut off.' He could see the future of the data-enabled business years earlier than most.

In his 1999 letter to shareholders, Bezos shared his vision for Amazon to become 'the everything store':

> Our vision is to use this platform to build Earth's most customer-centric company, a place where customers can come to find and discover anything and everything they might want to buy online.

> We'll listen to customers, invent on their behalf, and personalize the store for each of them, all while working hard to continue to earn their trust. Each new product and service we offer makes us more relevant to a wider group of customers and can increase the frequency with which they visit our store.[99]

---

99 https://www.cbinsights.com/research/bezos-amazon-shareholder-letters/.

AMAZON CULTURE OF EXPERIMENTATION

It is not possible in this book to provide a customised journey for every different type of organisation or reader, but this chapter can provide a framework for how you can work out your own journey, whether you head a small business, are an executive or board member in a large corporate, not-for-profit, government agency, start-up or scale-up.

Building a data culture

Watch out for HiPPOs – the highest paid person's opinion

The HiPPO can be the enabler of the large-scale adoption of data and AI like Jeff Bezos was back in his day or the barrier to the new way. Board's major responsibility is to ensure the CEO of the day is optimal for that organisation, at that time, and for the foreseeable future. Unfortunately, we have seen this go horribly wrong over and over again leading to some monumental failures. As reported in the *Harvard Business Review*:

> In most organizations, authority for the most important strategic decisions is left to the highest-paid person's opinion (HiPPO). All too often, the HiPPO can prove to be wrong. A HiPPO drove the strategy for JC Penny's disastrous move to go upmarket and abandon its thrifty customer base.[100]

---

100 https://hbr.org/2016/02/the-antidote-to-hippos-crowd-voting.

HiPPOs are also responsible for the downfall of many once great organisations. The notion that no one is as smart as everyone occurs even in the C-suite.

An organisational culture of data-driven decision-making is where evidence and reason flow throughout the organisation, where the quality of the data underpins trust and reliability and where a values-based approach to governance is at the forefront of all decisions.

A data culture is where data is treated as a valuable asset, and where the customer interest is sacrosanct

It's also important to share what a data culture is not. A culture is holistic, not partial, so it's not about undertaking a digital transformation in one part of your business, most likely the customer interface. That is a 'project'.

Thomas H Davenport wrote the following in the *HBR*:

> I'm convinced that the ingredient for the effective use of data and analytics that is in shortest supply is managers' understanding of what is possible. Data, hardware, and software are available in droves, but human comprehension of the possibilities they enable is much less common. Given that problem, there is a great need for more education on this topic.

Recent analysis of digital transformations observed that successful projects exhibited a 70:20:10 ratio. Seventy per cent of the effort went on process, ways of working, people issues and KPIs, 20% went on getting the data right, and 10% was on the technology. The research also noted that as most businesses are still really product-led and not customer-led, the effort by executives needs to happen first to change the way the business orients from the product being paramount, to the customer being at the centre of their purpose.[101]

When data transformation is technology-led or data-led, you miss the real opportunity for change.

If you're not a digital native, you need to make a serious effort to upskill and learn as much as you can about data, AI and machine learning. Reading this book is a good start, but you also need to engage with the data leaders in your organisation, ask lots of questions and get curious. If you're a start-up it's easier for you to build your organisation with a data spine; in fact, there's a high likelihood that your start-up is founded on data, AI and machine learning.

If you're the executive of a legacy business and/or a bricks-and-mortar business, you need to stand back from the fear of the onslaught coming from your global data/AI competitors to reimagine your business model.

---

101 Customer Experience in the *Age of AI, Harvard Business Review*, March /April 2022.

Getting started with your AI/data journey

As is often the case, eventually the pain of inaction will intensify to the point where action is less painful.

If your inertia about your fitness program continues long enough there will eventually be a day where you need to move more because it is lifesaving. It is the same for organisational adoption of data and AI enablement. The early days are hard, ambiguous, even dangerous, with cost blowouts and organisational frustration. It is like that at the start, just like the first morning at the gym after a lifetime of sitting at a desk. Stop and you will pay a very high price.

There's an old joke that encapsulates how many executives and business owners feel about the data/AI revolution. A couple from the city get lost when out on a drive in the countryside and ask a farmer for directions back to town. 'Oh, I wouldn't start from here,' the farmer replies with a grin.

So, just where do you start if you haven't already? And if you have, you might want to take a brief pause and ask yourself the following questions.

1. Where are you now?
2. Where do you want to be?
3. How will you get there?
4. What are the forces that are driving the change?

1. Where are you – really?

In Michael Lewis's book, *The Premonition*, about the global pandemic, he recounts that before the Covid-19 pandemic started, a group of health experts from around the world were paid a lot of money to assess the world's capability to deal with a pandemic. They ranked every country's capacity to handle a pandemic, and guess what? America was ranked the most prepared country in the world – the most organised, with the highest capability, best doctors and most resources. Of course, when the pandemic hit, America did not shower itself in glory in its performance compared to other developed nations in terms of avoidable deaths.

This summary struck me as completely relevant to executives assessing where their company is in terms of their data/AI use and capability, because when you're assessing yourself it's easy to compare your company to others in your sector and become complacent. Just like the US pandemic expert panel who assessed the USA's capability as high on a set of metrics that didn't take into account the real-world impacts of the virus, political interference, bureaucratic blunders, misinformation on social media and the politicisation of health advice. Understanding the real issues around your organisation's ability to assess your AI and data capability is harder than it seems.

An honest appraisal of your current data situation and capability to capture, share, interpret and action it is essential. Before you make any decisions, ask for a briefing (either from an internal or external team if you have these roles) to understand just where your business is in terms of what data you have, where it's held, how it's shared (if at all), what is its purpose, who is responsible for its quality, security and governance.

It may well be a good idea to get an external party, a data AI specialist, to assess your current status. Auditors assess the current financial status, and provide an independent view of the processes and team in the finance department, so there is value in an independent data view.

INDICATIVE VIEW OF AI AND DATA STRENGTH
WHERE DO YOU RANK?

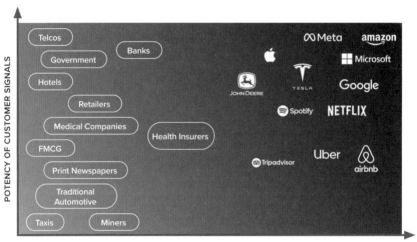

CAPABILITY TO USE CUSTOMER SIGNALS

Illustrative at time of publishing, noting that there are clearly examples of banks, telcos, FMCG and the like who are great users of customer signals

You must understand your data and the opportunities and threats that exist in its storage and use

If you're in a large company, typically the executives and board members will ask the people running customer experience, marketing and sales about their data, as this is where most customer data sits. If you have a chief data officer, they are likely to be the first point of contact and, if your company is highly attuned to the power of data, your chief risk officer will also be a key person to engage. Ericsson, who has built global telecommunications networks, has a data enablement officer.[102]

Ask your customers to rank your company's capability to predict their needs. Ask them to compare you to some of your competitors and, more importantly, how you compare to the more progressive users of data.

Benchmarking the performance of the company against the leaders in other more customer-centric industries could be illuminating. For example, if you are an energy company and benchmark yourself against banks, the results might show that you perform okay, and that you're ahead of banks. Now that Apple has banking products, the status quo will be challenged. However, I'd suggest you benchmark your company against Netflix or Etsy, advanced digital companies. Your new AI-data-driven competitor will be thinking about how to create the Netflix of your sector and that is when you will feel the full force of data-driven competition.

Fortunately, there's an increasing cohort of C-suite executives who understand the importance of data and AI and are capable of assessing their own company's vulnerabilities and are taking decisive action to try and change it. This pool of talent is in very high demand, and we need a larger pool of expertise here. Indeed, a key reason for this book is to shed more light on this need and develop the necessary expertise.

2. Where do you want to be?

'The most reliable way to forecast the future is to try to understand the present.' – John Naisbitt

Denial of change is not a strategy, predicting the customers' needs is. A question I am asked a lot is, 'If you were in our business with what you know about data, what would you suggest we do?' My response is: 'Try to imagine what the future looks like for your customers. Surround yourself with all the customer information that you can possibly get because you're basically looking to find the unmet needs of your customers today and tomorrow.'

What would you do if you could understand every possible customer need? There's a story about Apple's App Store. When Apple was launching the iPhone, Steve Jobs was not keen on the concept of the App Store. One of his lieutenants said, 'We've got to have this store, it's going to drive demand for the phones.' Jobs was not convinced and reiterated that he thought the best thing was to just put the phone out as it had the web in the browser form.

---

102 How a tech company went from moving data to using data: An Interview with Ericsson's Sonia Boije, McKinsey Digital, October 2021, pdf.

After further discussions he acquiesced and agreed to have the App Store.

If Steve Jobs couldn't see the power of the App Store when he designed the iPhone, you're not alone if there are opportunities and risks you can't see before you get to a data- and AI-enabled business.

The typical CFO/CEO/board wants to see a three-to-one payback on the first AI-data initiative. The reality is that's unlikely to happen from the get-go. Starting will include the friction of data sorting, enabling, testing, and the best business case is unlikely to be your first. I have seen paybacks of over forty-to-one from longer-term data initiatives. What other activity have you invested in recently that paid back like this? Now that AI can be reprogrammed and increasingly rebuilt, the ROI will grow from a baseline that is already high.

I had a memorable meeting with the CEO of a large business who said, 'We don't need to do all this data stuff as we have revenue growth and it's going well.' I asked him this question: 'Do your shareholders know that the organisation is reluctant to invest in understanding its customers' needs and future needs?' That is the decision you are making, at the exact time that your customers' expectations are climbing, because they're only one click away from a company that can better serve them with what they want. Just out of interest, I looked up the share price of this business as I wrote this; it's down 80% and that same CEO was shown the door in a shareholder revolt a few years later.

An ongoing process

The taxi industry was decimated because they thought they understood the customer, and that the customer benefit was clear. Then, suddenly, it wasn't. Uber comes in followed by Ola, Didi, Lyft and more. Why did they disrupt the venerable taxi industry around the world? Their customer service was better, their customer engagement more seamless, they were cheaper (sometimes) and they keep on investing in research and development. Of course, I can't write about Uber without noting its various challenges, lack of profitability, and governance disasters. However, the point I am making here is that Uber, a company that started in 2009, grew to be the world's most valuable start-up and listed on the NYSE in 2019. It continues to invest in using data as its North Star.

Uber's research and development budget is enormous: $1.5b in 2017, $4.8b in 2018, $2.2b in 2019 and $1.9b in 2020.[103] They haven't said, 'Here's the best version of the app, so we're stopping.' They've said, 'Here's the best version of the app, and we're doubling down on research and development.'[104]

---

103 https://www.macrotrends.net/stocks/charts/UBER/uber-technologies/research-development-expenses.

104 https://www.investopedia.com/articles/personal-finance/111015/story-uber.asp.

3. How will you get there?

Just as you need to be able to undertake an honest appraisal of where you are now (aka no egos, HiPPOs, not-invented-here mindsets), you'll need to develop clear structures and systems that support a dynamic flow of information, insights, discussion and decision-making in radically different time frames than you are probably now working in. Embrace that you'll be receiving insights and ideas, and seeing opportunities that you hadn't even thought about.

Once you are truly on the data/AI journey you must be careful of the 'not-invented-here' syndrome as this can easily reduce the capacity of the business to develop, implement and scale your data-driven business. Instead, add a little 'proudly invented elsewhere', a concept that was shared with me by Citibank.

Develop, buy, borrow or partner

At the point you decide you have to act and grow as a data-driven business, you need to decide whether you develop your own team and algorithms, partner with a specialist company, or buy existing solutions. The answer may even be a combination of all three.

If you're a small business with limited resources, before you spend anything, look at what's available for free. Google has a myriad of tools that allow you to see searches in your category. A friend of mine has a small organic food start-up and asked for advice. Before I did anything else I searched Google Trends for my friend's food category. Queensland, surprisingly, had 100% more searches than NSW does with a larger population. That is free data, and helpful in this instance. Add to this, a listing of restaurants that sell that type of food and you can get an early view of where the market is and where the market is heading. It will export the searches to a spreadsheet, and my friend could start working on that immediately. This is real-time customer intention for free. It's all about taking the time to think of the questions that will set you up for success:

1. What is the total market for my product or service today? In five years from now?
2. Where is my market, by location?
3. What key attributes do my customers have? Age, income, lifestyle, other purchasing behaviours, which carefully avoid the King Charles and Ozzy Osbourne blunt segment conundrum.
4. What do they do when not using my product? (That is a very creative question that needs real data to answer, but it leads to some very powerful insights.)

5. What are my competitors offering them?

6. Does the customer notice the difference between my product and the competition's? How is it better?

7. What is the unmet need of new and existing customers that my products or services can fulfil?

8. What competitive response could occur that would make my plans fail?

9. What mitigation action can I take to develop a competitive response?

Without knowing your specific use case, industry and existing capability, it's not possible to give specific guidance on the build, buy or partner decision. What I would say is that almost all companies partner in legal and accounting, as it's complex and getting it wrong is a material threat. The partnerships are often also augmented with internal executives, like internal legal counsel or financial controllers. AI-data analytics is complex and getting it wrong is a material threat. Studies have shown that the top analytics talent produces outsized returns. The best data scientists and engineers are 10 to 50 times more productive than average performers. The lesson here is to make sure that if you are going in-house your team really is capable, and that, in turn, creates the challenge of who in the organisation is well equipped to evaluate the team or any external suppliers.

There will be failures and success – keep going

In a letter to shareholders, Jeff Bezos said, 'One area where I think we are especially distinctive is failure. I believe we are the best place in the world to fail (we have plenty of practice!), and failure and invention are inseparable twins.' He goes on to say that all breakthroughs come from failure.[105] If you're working in a very clinical, financially driven place with no culture of the art of the possible, you're probably going to struggle in driving your business through the data/AI revolution.

It's a continuous process, where the customer leads you rather than you second-guessing the customer.

---

105 https://www.cbinsights.com/research/bezos-amazon-shareholder-letters/.
https://www.gobankingrates.com/money/business/jeff-bezos-worst-business-failures/#:~:
text=%E2%80%9COne%20area%20where%20I%20think,and%20invention%20are%20
inseparable%20twins.%E2%80%9D.

4. What are the forces that are driving the change?

You can't be in a business anywhere in the world now where your customers aren't aware of what great analytics and AI looks like. Billions of customers use Apple, Amazon, Google, Spotify, Siri, Alexa, Alibaba, Tencent, Waze, TikTok and many more. A small dollar subscription spent on Netflix gives the user access to US$16 billion of content created based on the preferences (data) of other Netflix users. This is a very high-value proposition that all companies now compete with. Your customers know what good looks like and they expect it from you.

In August 2021 Australia's Federal Court handed down a decision that stated that 'an inventor can be non-human'. That is, they've decided that artificial intelligence can be legally recognised as the inventor in patent applications.[106] This means if you create some AI that you own, and if AI then invents a better way in five years' time, you own that as well. AI can create new assets which, in turn, can create new assets, which repeats endlessly. This is where AI: Game On companies are doubling down. What other investment can you make in your business that could have a perpetual reinvention of innovation and use? How do you price this investment now and how do you predict what its worth might be in the future? Is the normal ROI the right model? What is the value of Amazon's recommendation engine? You can mount a plausible argument that Amazon's cross-sell algorithm is worth hundreds of billions of dollars in value to Amazon. It makes them money while they sleep.

Tesla now has so much data coming back from each car – its capacity to understand the roads of Byron Bay, Boston or Bogotá – and this advantage accrues to them. In turn, they'll sell even more cars because the system is good and getting better as Tesla acquires more data. That's the virtuous cycle of data, or the flywheel of the data/data network effect.

In the next chapter I explore the types and flow of data within companies, expanding out from the focus on customers into how data and AI can be applied across companies in areas that many think are not or cannot be data-driven.

---

106 https://www.abc.net.au/news/2021-08-01/historic-decision-allows-ai-to-be-recognised-as-an-inventor/100339264.

CHAPTER TAKEAWAYS

1. Customers are judging the experiences they have with all organisations according to the standards they experience with the very best, and the best are typically advanced data-driven organisations.

2. Data is sustainable, and its life cycle includes refinement, reuse, blending, augmentation with other data, and remodelling for new use cases.

3. A data culture is where data is treated as a valuable asset, and where the customer interest is sacrosanct.

4. Successful digital transformations require a 70:20:10 ratio, where 70% of the effort goes into process, ways of working, people issues, and KPIs, 20% on getting the data right, and 10% on technology.

5. To become an AI data-driven business, companies must be honest in their appraisal of their current status, develop clear structures and systems for decision-making, embrace the possibility of receiving new insights and ideas, avoid the 'not-invented-here' syndrome, and consider developing, buying, borrowing or partnering for data-driven solutions.

Chapter 9

WHAT'S NEXT IN DATA AND AI

'In every decision, be it personal, governmental or corporate,
we must consider how it will affect our descendants seven generations
into the future.' – Seventh Generation Principle, Iroquois Nation

Boards are the ultimate custodian of the enterprise's future. How your organisation adapts to AI: Game On will decide its future. Every person and organisation will be affected by the seismic changes that AI is producing.

The trajectory of AI use is not always clear. Watson was IBM's AI hero more than a decade ago when it won the TV show *Jeopardy*. Soon there were claims Watson was working on new cancer research and other high-value use cases. IBM called Watson 'the future of knowing'. They had TV ads with Watson talking to Bob Dylan about his songwriting style and Watson was seen as an AI revolution in the making. The reality fell short.

Today's AI capabilities are more advanced, more democratised. That said, there will be hazards, setbacks and hype in some sectors. Leaders will need to be curious and have humility and scepticism.

In Chapter 1, I referenced Chris Anderson, editor of *Wired*, who said in 2008 that the 'sheer volume of data would obviate theory and even scientific method'.[107]

Now that we're in 2024, many more directors and executives across the commercial, environmental, health, medical, agriculture and energy fields are utilising the power of data and AI in their decision-making, business platforms, research and more.

---

107 https://www.wired.com/2008/06/pb-theory/.

Data and AI are changing and challenging how you think about how you think

Up until recently human beings have been the undisputed best source of knowledge, collectors of data and the instigators of most predictive capability in the known universe.

Our human software and hardware evolve achingly slowly – it's evolution, after all. Machines and AI are evolving at an exponential rate and as the expansion of data grows even faster, the compounding effects of machines writing better and faster code are accelerating at speeds we can't fully comprehend.

Today, humans are making more and more decisions directed and augmented by machines, and in doing so we are increasingly abdicating our decisions to these machines. Think about your average day. Your newsfeed, drive to work or commute on public transport, the weather, TV show recommendations, and increasingly romantic potential partners are all outsourced to AI for many people. We hand off decision-making frequently, already, and it's growing fast. Some of our decision-making here will range from good, bad to ugly, and the use case and ethics of the providers will matter like never before. How will these boards and executives be deciding who or what decides is going to impact every person on the planet.

How do we decide who or what decides?

A *Wired* article in February 2023 titled 'The Age of AI Hacking Is Closer Than You Think' was subtitled 'Algorithms struggle to understand human ambiguity'. But such quirks are a flimsy shield against the threat of artificially intelligent hackers.

Bruce Schneier, a renowned security technologist, wrote the following:

> While a world filled with AI hackers is still a science-fiction problem, it's not a stupid science-fiction problem. Advances in AI are coming fast and furious, and jumps in capability are erratic and discontinuous. Things we thought were hard turned out to be easy, and things we think should be easy turn out to be hard.
>
> We need to start thinking about enforceable, understandable, and ethical solutions, because if we can expect anything with AI, it's that we'll need those solutions sooner than we might expect.

Schneier went on to point out AI in the hands of the wrong people can be tasked with some very nefarious tasks. He used the example of aiming AI at tax laws looking for loopholes, resulting in thousands of new loopholes being found. Society is simply not ready for what could be done here. Hackiing up until now has been done by individuals – we are entering a time when it can be done and created by machines.[108]

Some questions to keep in mind on this journey:

- When do we delegate to the machine?
- When do we step in to take 100% human control?
- What is the data we use when we decide to ignore the data from the machines? How are you going to audit the training data that led to the decision?
- Many organisations are now educating staff to make them aware that anything that goes into OpenAI is now available for anyone else. What is your plan to stop this drift of IP?
- What if a disgruntled employee of KFC put the secret 11 herbs and spices up on OpenAI? You get the point.

There are more questions:

- How do we govern the data sets of our decisions?
- What bias do we bring to the table or the machine?
- How do we assess our own bias and with what data?

Eric Schmidt suggests there are a few key themes that are driving the frontier of AI.

1. **Machines that can see.** Machines see better than people, from X-rays to driverless cars, and this computer vision is changing athlete management. Using facial recognition, managers can use real-time analysis of their athletes during games to sharpen training plans and help avoid injuries. Mustard, a baseball app, is one current example that employs this computer vision, while Liverpool Football Club uses AI-driven data analytics and 10 US figure skaters used a system called 4D motion at the 2022 Winter Olympics.[109]

2. **Deep learning.** One of the more famous examples of AI in recent years was when the machine defeated the world's best AlphaGo players, using some new moves and strategies that had never been used by humans across more than 2,500 years of playing the game.

---

108 https://www.wired.com/story/artificial-intelligence-hacking-bruce-schneier/.

109 How AI could help predict – and avoid – sports injuries, Eric Niiler, *The Wall Street Journal*, 4 June 2022.

3. **Predictive computer models.** The use of AI for pharmaceutical drugs has helped changed the field, leading to new non-resistant antibiotics: 'Screening is not new, but until now, these models were not sufficiently accurate to transform drug discovery. Previously, molecules were represented as vectors reflecting the presence or absence of certain chemical groups. However, the new neural networks can learn these representations automatically, mapping molecules into continuous vectors which are subsequently used to predict their properties.'

At MIT, computer scientists and synthetic biologists achieved a very complicated experiment, using 100 million different compounds to figure out which ones would create a reaction for antibiotic use. Using this technique, they came up with a new drug called Halicin. So far, Halicin looks to be the next broad-scale antibiotic – the first of its kind in roughly four years.[110]

The generative AI sector is thriving, with billions of ventures forming to capitalise on OpenAI and other technology. Writing, music, art, business, science and more are going to be influenced by this type of technology. There are already platforms available including Jasper, Simplified and ContentBot that offer different versions of generative AI. For example, OpenAI's DALL-E 2 creates high-resolution concept art from text commands, while when it comes to coding AI is having a major impact. In November 2021, a third of the code on GitHub (a hosting platform for code) was being written with Copilot, a GPT-3 tool that had been created only five months previously.[111]

With the size of deep learning models increasing exponentially they will impact and transform every part of scientific research and discovery we know.

As we head to a future that will be enabled with data, fed into AI at increasing speed, we are going to need real care in our governance.

As an organisation, if you start with the premise that the system should be designed so that it optimises along the data Hippocratic oath first, and do no harm, you will be starting in a good place.

Just because you can does not mean you should. As an example, double parking is bad for traffic flow, but it is tolerated in small doses for emergencies. We don't condone speeding, yet we don't track every car and give them an automatic ticket every time they go above the limit. Technically that would be easy. If you want to eliminate the vast majority of crime in our society, put cameras in every public space with face recognition, link it to the electoral roll

---

110 https://news.mit.edu/2020/artificial-intelligence-identifies-new-antibiotic-0220.

111 Danny's workmate is called GPT-3, James Purtill, https://apple.news/Aq_3SVHmzR5u_1gY9WJt VAA.

of the country, as well as all visitors to the country, and for every incident you get a facial ID. That is not hard to do, but in Australia we don't want it. But if you really care about crime, to the exclusion of personal freedom, it could be done. So, technology, AI and machine learning give us these choices and they are not choices that computer scientists should make. These are choices for society.

The cultural norms around the world are very different. Let's use surveillance cameras as an example. In Britain, they're widely accepted. If you're on the street, you're on camera. In the United States, there's partial coverage. Sometimes you are on camera; sometimes you're not. But in Germany, with the collective memory of the Stasi, the population is violently opposed to such surveillance. These three different democracies have made different choices in relation to surveillance camera deployment and use through public dis-cussion, protests and voting. What level of surveillance would you be prepared to accept for yourself or your children? The answers to this and other questions are often deeply complex as they relate to the balance between personal responsibility, community responsibility and standards, as well as what we are prepared to cede to the state or a global tech platform, or both.

I do not think that computer scientists, tech industry leaders and professionals should make these decisions, especially if you read my chapter about the ethics around data. Boards, tech industry leaders, professionals and computer scientists should engage the wider population and explain more clearly and transparently that many of today's tools, AI and other systems give all of us a range of choices.

> In China, a law was introduced in 2019 that banned minors from playing video games between 10 pm and 8 am, or from playing more than 90 minutes on a weekday. On 1 June 2021 every game in the country was required to add a new authentication system that checks a player's Chinese national identity (including their age) to help block underage players from going past those limits in the name of preventing video game addiction. As a result, Tencent, the biggest game company in the world, is rolling out facial recognition technology that will likely scan many gamers' faces every single evening, aiming to catch minors breaking a gaming curfew and help prevent video game addiction. [112]

---

112 https://www.theverge.com/2021/7/9/22567029/tencent-china-facial-recognition-honor-of-kings-game-for-peace.

The future is already here

We're seeing this play out in the world of business, government and research where there's a bifurcation of those that use AI well, namely the large tech giants of the world, and everybody else, who are yet to fully understand it. The challenge for companies that lag behind in the data/AI race is that once your competitors (or even companies that you didn't perceive as your competitors) have the data/AI advantage, this advantage keeps accruing to them exponentially, as they can now create more AI and accelerate even faster. This flywheel effect makes it difficult or near impossible for others, perhaps you and your company, to catch up.

The Canadian philosopher and founding father of media theory Marshall McLuhan argued in his seminal work *Understanding Media: The Extensions of Man* that the 'medium is the message', that the way humans absorb information remoulds who we are as individuals and as a society. McLuhan said that the shocking TV footage of the JFK assassination was the start of TV news becoming a big deal. Up until that moment news was for newspapers. Once you see that terrible moment, you realise no newspaper can really cover the news like that. Communication technology changes society. AI use is similar, in that it is now a medium and a message in one. Once you see real personalisation selected for you, real text-to-image applications, and conversations output in databases and the like, you can't go back to the old world. The change is impossible to reverse.

The cost to sequence a whole human genome has declined from $3 billion in 2003 to around $500 today – 5 X what a Moore's law trendline would dictate. The time required to sequence a genome is also plummeting. The first genome took 13 years of computing power, and now only requires a few hours of it. As costs have declined and computing power has increased, the number of human-genome base pairs sequenced per US dollar has soared (see chart below). DNA sequencing costs will continue to decline. By 2025, or sooner, the cost to sequence a human genome will drop to $100. However, the cost will keep declining to the equivalent of 'one delivery pizza', and ultimately to less than one cent per genome – the price of flushing a toilet.

COST **PER HUMAN GENOME**

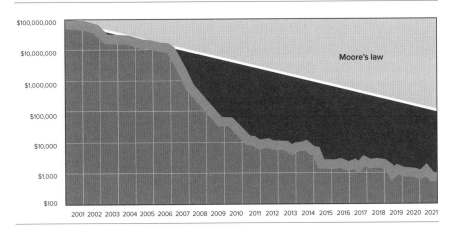

Source: National Human Genome Research Institute
https://www.genome.gov/about-genomics/fact-sheets/Sequencing-Human-Genome-cost.

Screening newborns is also a new frontier, as Raymond McCauley, chair of Digital Biology, explained back in 2017:

> As costs continue to fall, it may become standard practice to sequence the genomes of new-borns. We're going to be, as a matter of course, sequencing infants' DNA and predict the things that this human being is likely to face. We'll know what to worry about in the first 72 hours, then the first 6 months, then the first 3 years, then what we tell them when they turn 18.[113]

This is a road map to the prediction of many health issues for the individual. It's a worthy debate to be had. Do you want to know your chances of getting skin cancer in later life or not? If you did know your risks, would you change lifestyle factors to help lower risk? If you knew the risks for your children would you treat them differently?

There is a lot of conjecture about the way AI will lower operational costs in organisations, via increases in productivity and replacement of some jobs. AI seems to have deflationary capability and how this plays out will be fascinating. As the world's demographics age, particularly in developed countries, where natural population growth is declining, AI use may well turn out to be a power-ful addition to GDP growth.

I've written this book to help business leaders (in the broadest sense) think about what else could be predicted in their business and market for their customers as we are now in AI: Game On. The market for genetic-testing

---

113 Digital Biology, https://www.youtube.com/watch?v=TRxbH-t6mVM.

services is projected to be more than $17 billion by 2026. This is a new prediction industry in health. What is your current business and what could or must be your future business, based on an AI: Game On approach? What data is available in your business right now and outside it to do this?

AI and its impact on everything

'Artificial Intelligence is the new electricity.'
— Professor Andrew Ng

Google CEO Sundar Pichai notes that the impact of AI will be even greater than that of fire or electricity on our development as a species. So caution is needed now.

When and if a machine can outthink humanity, and out-predict our needs, the world becomes a riskier place. Any machine that can think and predict human needs and intentions needs to do so in a way that is aligned with humanity's interests. Who has the right to own such a machine?

If the machine acts away from humanity's best interest, it drifts into the world of rogue machine behaviours, which has been dystopian sci-fi bread and butter for generations. Some of the brightest minds have credibly called out this risk, from Elon Musk to the late Stephen Hawking. If the AI-enabled prediction machines cannot be understood in what and how they are predicting, it all can go wrong. The purpose needs to be firmly earthed in the benefits for people. The Frankenstein dilemma of the creation that did not obey its master could be upon us. Pretending this is not a possibility is naive, and working to ensure it does not occur is our responsibility.

We will be facing challenges, ethics, AI-weaponised misinformation, illusions of trust in fake accounts and more. Generative AI can be a convincing parrot, sounding good and knowing little, if not used carefully.

There will be new ventures that are focused on taking out misinformation, taming the troll farms; there will be new ideas and we need them. My son has an idea about how to verify human input into music and art. Andi Search has ways of showing the source documents it uses for summaries to take out the hallucinations that occur in some other forms of AI.

Your business has a data asset that is not going to be found in OpenAI. It's your propriety data to create value for your customers, stakeholders and society.

Every industry sector, every area of science, technology, medicine, health, the climate, resources, culture, finance, the arts … are being impacted by data/AI and machine learning. New businesses, different business models, new approaches, new or different solutions are emerging every day.

The world is a complex, dynamic and challenging place. Volatility, uncertainty, complexity and ambiguity (VUCA) are all around us and expanding in all aspects of life.

AI may one day reduce some of this VUCA. But that is not what is here now. AI is adding to VUCA at exponential rates. AI is too big to ignore, too complex to fully delegate, changing too fast to be fully comprehensible. At the same time, business leaders are accountable for what to do with AI, how to plan, what ethics to adopt, and what use cases to pursue. Stand still and a new entrant or existing competitor launches a new AI-enabled product or service that could damage your business. Go too fast and you overstep what are deemed acceptable use cases.

Businesses, society and individuals are facing much hardship. Climate change, large-scale income inequality, changing geopolitical forces, the war on Ukraine, new spheres of influence, just to name a few. Data, analytics and AI can and are being used to help solve some of these issues and in an ethical way.

The amount of change in our world will never be this slow again. Moore's law, advances in quantum computing (including the recent breakthrough by the Australian company Silicon Quantum Computing [SQC] that announced the world's first integrated circuit manufactured at the atomic scale)[114] and other compounding effects ensure today is the slowest rate of change you will ever see. The use of AI and data will accelerate faster than our imagination can predict. It's time for business leaders to embrace what is possible in a responsible way that ensures humanity's future is bright.

I conclude this book with an optimistic outlook, realistic about the challenges we face with how AI will be used in our world and conscious of just how much is not predicable here.

It is clear just how much there is to learn, and how no one has all the answers, and much of what I have tried to convey in this book is open for debate. We are all trying to figure out the right way to help the world adapt to the AI: Game On point in time, and in a way that works for humanity. I have seen how data/AI can be a powerful force for good. I have seen that business leaders, executives and entrepreneurs can play a substantive role in solving some of our largest challenges and, in doing so, help the people of the world live better, more fulfilled lives.

---

114 https://www.minister.industry.gov.au/ministers/husic/media-releases/quantum-breakthrough-fuel-australian-industry#:~:text=Today%20the%20Australian%20quantum%20computing,developing%20silicon%2Dbased%20quantum%20computing.

It is also clear that if the use case is not aligned with society's best interests AI can do real harm, potentially on a large scale. It has the power to do that today and that power will grow. Are we on the verge of all having personal agents finding truth, acting on our behalf without bias and bringing it home to us? Or are we heading for more AI-enabled misinformation? Will our health bots find us optimal well-being and cures for diseases? Or will there be some dystopian world of machines coming our way? Shakespeare tells us that the rarer action is in virtue than in vengeance, so we cannot assume good will prevail. It needs people to fight for it, it needs regulators to act. Whatever happens, your organisation will need to be part of this new world where it is AI: Game On.

The world needs legal and ethical frameworks, viable well-understood guard rails, and we need leaders who have knowledge and expertise in these matters.

How to decide who or what decides is the question of our time.

CHAPTER TAKEAWAYS

1. In the same way that Marshall McLuhan claimed that the 'medium is the message' so too is AI fundamentally transforming the way society communicates and interacts. AI is the medium and message that can also take action, and at close to the speed of light.

2. Most organisations are likely to have a unique, proprietary data set that can be strategically enhanced to create insights and predictive capability.

3. Society should decide on levels of surveillance and data use, not just tech industry leaders and professionals.

4. The future of AI is unevenly distributed, and the tech giants maintain a significant advantage over others.

5. While AI may eventually help reduce uncertainty and volatility it would be wise to expect the pace of change will only accelerate for the foreseeable future.

FURTHER READING

The Hype Machine: How Social Media Disrupts Our Elections, Our Economy, and Our Health – and How We Must Adapt, Sinan Aral, Currency, 2021.

Who Can You Trust?: How Technology Brought Us Together and Why It Might Drive Us Apart, Rachel Botsman, Public Affairs, 2017.

Post Corona, From Crisis to Opportunity, Scott Galloway, Bantam Press, 2020.

Leadering: The Ways Visionary Leaders Play Bigger, Nancy Giordano, PBI Publishing, 2021.

Homo Deus: A Brief History of Tomorrow, Yuval Noah Harari, Harper Perennial, 2018.

The Inevitable: Understanding the 12 Technological Forces That Will Shape Our Future, Kevin Kelly, Penguin, 2017.

Leadership: Six Studies in World Strategy, Henry Kissinger, Allen Lane, 2022.

Select Committee on Artificial Intelligence, Lord Clement-Jones (Chairman), https://publications.parliament.uk/pa/ld201719/ldselect/ldai/100/10001.htm.

The Premonition: A Pandemic Story, Michael Lewis, W W Norton & Company, 2021.

Further listening

'PIVOT', Scott Galloway and Kara Swisher
https://podcasts.apple.com/au/podcast/pivot/id1073226719.

INDEX